MUMMING

Victoria Vanstone is a comedy writer and host of the award-winning podcast *Sober Awkward*.

Originally from Reading in the UK, she now resides on Australia's Sunshine Coast with her annoyingly nice husband 'Poor John', her dog Sandy, and three sticky, loud, but occasionally delightful, children.

When she's not shouting into the abyss or aggressively typing, you'll find her crawling under the kitchen table retrieving dropped spaghetti, storming down the beach on her daily rage walk, or sitting in the Aldi car park, sobbing into a family-sized bag of chips.

Victoria is also the author of *A Thousand Wasted Sundays*, a brutally honest (but wildly funny) memoir about her journey to sobriety. *Mumming* is her second book – solid proof that absolute chaos is, in fact, a writer's best friend.

MUMMING

VICTORIA VANSTONE

PANTERA
PRESS

PANTERA
PRESS

First published in 2025 by Pantera Press,
an imprint of Hardie Grant Publishing

Pantera Press
Gadigal Country
Level 7, 45 Jones Street
Ultimo NSW 2007

Pantera Press acknowledges the Aboriginal Traditional Custodians of the Countries on which we work, and we pay our respect to Elders both past and present.

A Cataloguing-in-Publication entry for this book is available from the National Library of Australia.

ISBN 9780648618980 (Paperback)
ISBN 9780645858099 (eBook)

Cover design: Elysia Clapin
Cover images: © EyeEm Mobile GmbH/iStock by Getty Images, Say-Cheese/iStock by Getty Images, YesPhotographers/Shutterstock
Publisher: Katherine Hassett
Project editor: LinLi Wan
Editor: Kirsty van der Veer
Proofreader: Pam Dunne
Typesetting: Kirby Jones
Author photo: Carly Head

Printed in Australia by Opus Group Pty Ltd, an Accredited ISO AS/NZS 14001 Environmental Management System printer.

MIX
Paper | Supporting
responsible forestry
FSC **FSC® C018684**
www.fsc.org

The paper this book is printed on is certified against the Forest Stewardship Council® Standards. Griffin Press – a member of the Opus Group – holds chain of custody certification SCS-COC-001185. FSC® promotes environmentally responsible, socially beneficial and economically viable management of the world's forests.

For Mum and Dad
Sorry for throwing the rice pudding down the toilet.

'It's all crazy that we are all allowed to breed. I just can't get over it because none of us, with few exceptions, really know anything about it or what the hell we're doing.'

Larry David

Contents

Prologue

It All Started by the Side of a Road

When I was six my parents left my sister and me by the side of a road. We were in France on our way to the campsite we visited every summer. A place that smelt of pine trees, where grey-haired men played pétanque, metal balls gently tapping against one another in dappled sunlight as kids ran barefoot down dusty tracks that led to the ocean. We had stopped for petrol on the highway. When Mum and Dad went inside to pay and get some sweets for the journey, my sister and I got out of the car to go to the toilet. When we came back, they were gone.

The road stretched forever. I swivelled on my feet. Grit caught in my sandal from the gravel. My head turned in every direction. Nothing. Just people, faces I did not recognise. Over at the petrol pumps a farmer in a flat cap bent down over a jerry can. A lady sat in the front seat of a rusty blue car as a man filled up, his arm leaning on the roof. The door of the kiosk slammed closed every time a customer exited. Strangers coming and going with bags of snacks and canned drinks.

I shivered when I looked back at the road. Rain tickled my face. My big sister pulled my hood up over my head.

'Let's stay here,' she said. 'Let's just wait.'

Trucks rumbled past, cars whizzed by. I squeezed her hand and we stood, next to each other, on the side of a road.

I wasn't scared. I knew it was a mistake. Soon a car would come hurtling towards us and my mum would leap out, scoop us up and we'd get on with the holiday.

We stood there for an hour. Shoes filled with water; clothes stuck to our skin. My duffle coat got heavier with each passing moment. The smell of petrol filled our nostrils. I fiddled with a coin that had snuck through a hole in my pocket, sliding around in the lining of my coat.

Nobody came to see if we were okay. Nobody noticed the two little girls by the side of the road. We stood firm with nothing but certainty as the rain fell and the world carried on around us.

*

A few days before the big drive, my sister and I had shoved pillows and quilts into the back seat of my parents' old

Citroën, making a comfy camp for the journey. We were always creating little nooks and dens to hide in as kids. Sheets were hung from door frames with parcel string, cushions leant up against coffee tables creating secret entrances. We clambered over piles of shoes in the bottom of wardrobes and crouched under Mum's silky dresses, dust making our noses tickle. 'We're hiding! Come and find us!'

When my parents got back from paying for the petrol, they had peered into the back seat presuming we were there, hiding under one of the sleeping bags.

'Roger, have you seen Victoria? She must be around here somewhere?' Mum had said, thinking we could hear.

'No, I've not seen either of them. Maybe they don't want the jelly babies we just bought them …'

Unbeknown to them, we were not hiding this time.

By the time they realised we were missing they were halfway to Marseille.

'Come on kids, the joke's over, out you come …'

I can imagine the blood draining from Mum's face as she pulled back the sleeping bag to see our Walkmans and teddy bears discarded on the seat where we should have been curled up like a couple of pretzels, giggling.

*

I saw the UK numberplate first and then my mum's nose pressed up against the windscreen. Dad's face beside her, white against the darkness of the car. When she spotted us, standing in a puddle holding hands, her chin dropped to her chest. Her relief turned her body to jelly.

My mum fumbled with the door handle. She sprung out of the car before it came to a standstill. Lurched forward, grabbed us, and pulled us into her.

'We thought you were hiding.' She sobbed into my neck.

Over her shoulder I saw Dad in the driver's seat, his forehead resting on the steering wheel, bawling his eyes out.

'It's okay, Mummy. We weren't scared,' my sister said as she hugged Mum's trembling body. Dad got out of the car, came over and wrapped his arms around us.

We stayed like that for a while. A pillar of hats, coats and tears, cuddled up in the rain. Both my parents in need of a moment to process.

When we got back in the car, Dad started the engine and adjusted his rear-view mirror so he could see us in the back seat. I gave him a thumbs up and, as we sped towards the campsite, I watched the colour slowly return to his cheeks.

*

It didn't matter how long they left us there that day.

    We would have stood by that busy road forever.

    We knew they were coming back.

*

This isn't a book about perfect parenting. It's a book about always coming back.

'You're Fired!'

January 2024

I slide open the door of the brightly lit classroom. Colourful drawings of flowers flap on the walls as a gust of wind rushes in behind me. I walk towards a group of mums standing near a bubbling kettle. As I glance around the space, a toddler with a disturbing 'party at the back' mullet and snot streaming out of his nose catches my eye. He's sitting on his mum's lap, scoffing Cheezels. I give him a little wave and he flips the bird. I close my eyes and, like Dorothy in *The Wizard of Oz*, click the heels of my Birkenstocks together as I mutter, 'There's no place like home', hoping I might teleport to Kmart.

'Would you like a cup of tea before we get started?' A lady with dangly earrings that drop just beneath her jaw-length bob catches me backing towards the exit.

'Yes please!' I say, having noticed a plate of custard creams. If anything, they are worth staying for.

'There are pens and sticky labels on the table over there.'

She points to a low desk that has a small sign folded open next to a pencil case of biros. The sign reads:

Welcome to Sunny Days Parenting.

I go over and jot my name on a label, pop my bag under a chair and wait for my tea.

Above me, a string of paper-plate jellyfish hangs from the ceiling, the yarn tentacles tickling my forehead. I blow them off and look around. There are trays with names on them, bags slotted into a wooden shelf, tubs of blocks and a trunk of fancy dress costumes with tulle and sequins all shoved inside. The walls are covered in blobby, monster-like self-portraits, with names underneath. *Kayden, Joel, Molly ...* then *Frob*, which I know from the spelling is my Fred. I take a deep inhale. *Just get on with it, Vic.*

I want to run back out into the playground and pretend this never happened, but I have to stay, for Frob, my little Freddie. I swallow my pride (and a party quiche) and wait for the lady with the bobbed hair and nice earrings to teach me how to be a good mummy.

*

I hadn't started today knowing I was going to a parenting class. I started it like any other day: on my knees, holding a dustpan and brush, cleaning up what had spilt off three plastic *Paw Patrol* plates.

'Can you guys just keep your food on your bloody plates, please,' I shouted.

There was so much food scattered around me on the floor that I considered just emptying the scrapings onto a pizza base and serving it for dinner. As I collected squashed raisins (individually plucked out of the raisin toast), I daydreamed about inventing a child-friendly slop trough, a sort of food gutter, where my three children – George (twelve), Nell (eight) and Fred (five) – could all line up, shove their heads in and suck up the food.

I swept the last bits onto the metal pan. Soft, dangling feet banged against my forehead. If anyone could have seen me, mumbling to myself, scraggly hair, on all fours in my nightie with a dustpan full of soggy cornflakes, they probably would have called the authorities. With any luck I'd be hauled off to a secure unit. Free food, a straitjacket, padded walls and strong medication twice a day could be just the mini-break I needed.

'And what's this?' I asked, holding up a small bowl containing yoghurt, washing-up liquid, gherkins and dried apricots.

'Nell made a concoction for you Mum,' George said, without taking his eyes off the TV.

Urgh.

So, this is where I was at.

Crawling around my kitchen floor, daydreaming about treating my children like farm animals. I know it's not right, but I'd completely run out of options. My parenting toolbox was officially empty.

I walked directly over to my computer and googled the cost of a cattle prod. Before I had a chance to click *Buy Now,* the next issue arises.

'Mummy, I can't find my shoe,' said Fred.

I took a deep breath. I didn't want to be annoyed but I couldn't help it. It wasn't even the first lost item of the morning. There had already been a laptop case, a doll's arm and 'Snuggy' (my youngest's cuddly rag). Their constant stream of misplaced objects piled up on me like dirty dishes, teetering on the edge of my already frazzled emotions.

Deep inside me somewhere is the mother I wanted to be, the one that kneels, holds shoulders, looks her child in the eyes and says softly, 'Now, Fred, we're on the same team. We can figure this out together. Let's go on a treasure hunt and find your mysterious lost shoe.'

I know she's there but, like the shoe, I can't find her. She's been replaced with a cheaper version, a worn-out substitute.

It wasn't meant to be like this. Mumming, I mean.

I thought I'd love every moment, be patient, kind and spend my days reorganising bedrooms and ironing name tags onto school shirts. I wanted to be one of those mums who hums jolly tunes as she throws wooden toys into wicker baskets, sews up holes in socks and wears flouncy dresses with worn-out maternity knickers beneath. I wanted to know the best chewy chocolate-chip cookie recipe off by heart and wear oven gloves. But as the years have ticked by, I get the feeling that woman isn't going to show up. What has emerged from the depths of motherhood is a grumpy troll who throws plastic cups at walls.

It doesn't feel great not being who I expected. It's like when you're anticipating a delivery from Temu and you open the door to a smiling Jehovah's Witness. It's disappointing.

'For god's sake! Why can't you kids just take your bloody shoes off and put them in the cupboard? You're driving me mad!'

There was no build-up to my cacophony; I started loud. The words burst from my mouth before I had a chance to consider them.

Fred looked up at me. We both knew his shoe was at the park, damp from the overnight rain, upside down next to the swings. My anger about what is quite a minor setback in the grand scheme of things built like a bushfire in a strong wind, heating every part of me until my brain started to boil. The only way I know how to relieve it is to shout, or destroy any household object that stands in my path. The broom handle was already snapped in two and the whisk had been hurled into the garden somewhere.

So, I went into the bathroom and threw an empty shampoo bottle at the bath. This short, sharp action released any accumulated tension. It was completely irrational, yet immensely satisfying.

When I calmed down, I felt silly. Why was I getting so angry about such small things? Is this who I'd become?

I haven't always been a shouter. Before I had children, I had nothing to shout about. I was never angry enough that raising my voice was necessary. I've not shouted at a bus conductor, at a bank manager or even the evil lady at the post office who sneers every time I hand over incomplete passport documents.

I never really shouted at boyfriends, either. There were fallouts, the flinging of a few venomous insults and the occasional blubbery sob into an armpit, but no high-decibel screeching, no Motörhead-level uproar. I was more of a sulker. A girl who avoided dramatic confrontation as much as possible.

I was laid-back before I had kids. I was a traveller, a nomad who carried a rucksack full of mix tapes and stories on her back for ten years, someone who dawdled through life with nothing to worry about except tan lines and coconuts falling on my head. (And standing on a beach shouting at coconuts attracts the wrong sort of attention.) Back then, I never liked or hated anyone enough for me to shout. If someone annoyed me, I'd just get on a bus and leave them behind. But it turns out that – even though some days I want to – you can't really do that with children.

If shouting was my only issue, I could probably just stick in some earplugs and survive the next eighteen years … But it's not.

I buy Kinder Eggs to keep them quiet at the shops. I never follow through with consequences. I'm inconsistent. I reward bad behaviour and I swear too fucking much. And now I'm stuck, like a toddler with their bum in a bucket – no way out without a helping hand.

*

My parenting burnout isn't sudden. It's been building for years. A slow, relentless grind of frustration. And I think it's my fault. I've taken the easy way out, brushing off parenting mishaps instead of fixing them. I've patched up family fights with flimsy band-aids that peel off as fast as I stick them on. No lessons learnt, no growth, just the same problems bubbling back up, repeatedly.

I have no idea where to start getting better at being a mum, but hating the sound of my own voice and scaring my kids daily is uncomfortably close to rock bottom. Something has to be done. It's time to leave the head-twisting *Exorcist* act behind, slip on my fluffy slippers, and take charge. No more slamming doors or making up rules as I go. No more winging it. This is my year-long mission; to hunt down the tools and strategies I need to get it right. I want to learn how to be a strong role model, not a mum who's barely holding it together.

*

I cleaned up the rest of the breakfast mess, wiped down the surfaces and found some rubber diving shoes in the shed for Fred. I convinced him the teachers wouldn't notice and somehow I got everyone into the car. Miraculously, we made it into school on time. Nell and George trundled up the path towards their classrooms and I took Fred's hand and headed over to the prep room. He'd been hard work all morning, not listening and not helping. I felt a bit guilty that I was looking forward to dropping him off.

Fred put his water bottle in the slot with his name and pulled his lunchbox out of his bag. I leant down for a kiss and he looked up at me and said, 'You're fired!'

'What? You can't fire me! I'm your mother!' He then dawdled off into the classroom, without saying goodbye. Instead of feeling proud and teary like the other mums there, all I thought was, *He's gone. Thank fuck for that.*

I walked back to the school carpark and looked up to see a mum I knew running towards me. She caught up, a little short of breath, and shoved a leaflet into my hand. I looked at it. On the front was a picture of a man carrying a laughing child on his shoulders. The title read:

Sunny Days Parenting. Stronger relationships for a better future.

'It starts today at eleven-thirty in the empty prep classroom. I hope you can make it, Vic.' Her eyes narrowed as she waited for an answer. It was a knowing face, one that told me she'd seen my mini-manager, wearing diving shoes, giving me the heave-ho.

I flashed back to my morning and was reminded how desperate I'd been to change.

I didn't want to go to the class, but I knew I had to.

I needed help.

'Will there be morning tea?'

'Yes, and you get a free pen.'

'Okay, I'll come.'

*

And now here I am, taking baby steps towards change.

Everybody makes their way over and sits down. There are four mums and one dad. We are all handed a workbook and told to select a picture from the cards spread out on the table.

'Choose the one that best depicts how parenting is going for you right now.'

I scan the images. A mother duck ushering some ducklings on a zebra crossing, a family of happy squirrels in hats all sitting at a dinner table and a goat at the wheel of a truck, stuck in mud, with three dirt-flecked baby goats in the back. My hand bangs into the lady next to me as we both reach to grab the dirty goats.

It's then I realise I am among my people. I give her a stupid smile and place the card between us. Two mums wading through the muck together.

I sit for three hours in a kid-size chair, asking questions and taking notes. Everyone is honest and open about their struggles. One mum is having issues getting her daughter to eat any veggies, one has a kid who answers back. The dad says his son won't get ready for school and the lady with snotty boy says, 'I make mine scrub the dunny when they're naughty.' I mentally add scrubbing brush under cattle-prod to my shopping list.

The cheerful school chaplain comes for an hour and teaches us about instilling morals in our kids. She gets out a transparent folder that holds laminated squares with words printed in large font and sticks twenty of them to the whiteboard with Blu Tack.

'Pick out three values that describe your children.'

I stare at the words. It takes me a while to choose. I'm so mixed up in anger and shouting that saying something nice about my children feels unnatural.

I get up from my chair and pick *Creative, Kind* and *Helpful*. (Only because *Selfish, Annoying* and *Thoughtless* aren't there.) An image of my daughter, Nell, doing craft at the dining room table pops into my mind, and as I walk back to my seat holding my chosen pieces of guillotined A4, I hold back tears.

I've been so busy shouting that I've forgotten how to be nice.

During the rest of our first class, we learn better coping tactics, do a short quiz on 'emotional guidance' and then watch a YouTube clip of a guy who looks like Jerry Springer talking about 'Start Behaviours' and a counting method to use when kids don't listen.

'Our aim this week is to teach ways to encourage healthy behaviours with your children,' he explains in a deep southern drawl. 'When your child is doing something undesirable, such as not listening, not following directions, whining, begging, crying, having a tantrum, all you say is "That's three." If your child does not do as you ask, then … that's a two. You keep counting until one and then if the behaviour has not changed they lose a privilege. This could mean an earlier bedtime or not having that visit to the water park at the weekend. Eventually they will stop their negative behaviour and you don't have to even get to number two.'

The lady with the nice earrings then pauses the video and says, 'A key element of Sunny Days Parenting is the "no talking, no emotion" rule. This means that when you are using counting-down as discipline, you do not talk, explain or rationalise with your child, and you do not get angry or otherwise emotional during or after.'

It was straightforward. I can count down from three, no problemo, and not talking, explaining or rationalising with my children would free up so much time. Maybe I had been overthinking mumming all along and it was simpler than I had imagined. It was just a numbers game and a matter of ignoring them when they are naughty. Brilliant. I make a note in my diary, *start the counting thing tonight*, and feel hopeful for the rest of the class.

I soak it all up, and as I pack my folder into my bag, I promise to replace the ogre that lives inside me with a more peaceful mummy. A mummy who doesn't swear or pull off Barbie heads. Doesn't put the gaming controller in the dustbin, threaten adoption twice a day or shout like an injured swamp donkey every time she finds toast crust in her bed.

'Thanks,' I say to the lady as I leave, 'I've enjoyed today.'

'Will you come next week? We are going to look deeper into those values, Vic.'

'Yes, I will be here.' My voice cracks. 'I know I can do better.'

'Don't worry. Just try to remember why you wanted to be a mum in the first place.'

I stand there for a while … not able to remember why.

The Hamster Feeder

When I get home, I stick the values I chose during the class on the fridge and add some extra ones. Respect, honesty, gratitude, love and tolerance. As I place them, one by one, I know it's not only the children who need to learn them.

Nell comes in. 'What are you doing?'

'I'm just going to try and be a little bit better at being your mummy.'

She pulls a sticker off the fridge. 'What are these for?'

'These are to remind us to be nice to each other.'

That night, after dinner, I explain the counting method. 'If I get to one it means you lose a privilege. I hope this tactic will mean I don't have to raise my voice with you lot anymore.' They roll their eyes at one another.

But I don't let their lack of faith put me off. I pack my worksheets in a little plastic folder and while they eat dessert, I download a parenting app. It offers an 'emergency de-stress tool' to be played when I feel like shouting. So, I stick in my headphones, hide in the pantry and do a six-minute guided unwind session that I hope will result in all our household utensils staying intact.

Then it's time for my next challenge: bedtime.

I imagined bedtime with kids would be like an episode of *The Waltons*. All my little angels tucked in bed with polite goodnights ricocheting around the house.

'Goodnight, John Boy.'

'Goodnight, Mamma.'

Unfortunately, the Waltons were fucking liars. The only sounds that bounce around my house are slamming doors, shrill cries of 'I'M NOT TIRED!' and the thud of my own feet as I march between bedrooms. Our sleep routine falls apart quicker than shortcrust pastry. In fact, sleep, my lack of it, other people's opinions on it, and my children's excuses not to do it, have ruled my life since I first heard that newborn cry.

Before I had my first child, I couldn't understand why a baby's sleep was so important. It's not like they had to get up for work in the morning, were going to miss a flight or had an important meeting with a mortgage broker. Who cares if they sleep or not? When George was born, I was blasé about routines. He was like a uni student for the first six weeks, only waking to eat and stare at ceiling fans. Just a little pink blob in a knitted hat. I made confused expressions as the other mums complained about 'the nights' while my little gnome snoozed in his car capsule beside me. A friend once made me poke him awake, to prove he wasn't one of those 'reborn' fake baby dolls. He opened one eye as if to say, 'Leave me alone. I'm not ready to be out yet, Mummy!'

Then, it happened. One fateful day, he woke up and didn't ever want to sleep again.

I paced the house at night holding my wailing boy with no idea what to do.

'You look tired, Vicky. Just give him some cough mixture.' My mum was on the phone giving me a high dose of bad advice.

'But he doesn't have a cough?'

'It doesn't matter. It'll knock him out. You should take some too. I would. You'll both sleep like rocks.'

'I'm going to try co-sleeping. It's what they do in Japan.'

'Dad asks, have you tried taping his mouth up with duct tape? That's what he used to do to you.' She giggled.

'I hope you're joking, Mum.'

'I've got to go, Lyn's here with a pavlova.'

When George was six months old, I got so fed up with my parents asking, 'Is he sleeping through?' that I bought a hamster feeder, filled it with formula and attached it to his cot, purely to make it look like I had found a solution. I FaceTimed them in France and filmed the contraption in the background, fixed onto one of the slats.

'Look, they have these new devices where babies help themselves to milk throughout the night.' My parents were astonished.

'Bloody genius. Why did no one think of this in my day?'

I was pleased my lie shut them up, but it didn't actually solve my problem. That boy cried so loud for so long that his face turned as red as a tomato. I thought he might explode. Nothing I did pacified him. (And I used the last bit of duct tape fixing my reading glasses.) I didn't know where to turn, and everyone, including the postman, my mother-in-law, Mary from the café, and scary Jenny from the maternity unit, had an opinion on sleep.

'Never wake a sleeping baby.'

'Put him on his side.'

'Put him on his back.'

'Give him a dummy.'

'I used to swaddle mine, worked a treat.'

'Put the pram in the garden, let him get a bit of sun.'

I did put him in the garden once, but I lived on the second floor of an apartment block and the people partying in the communal area didn't appreciate a screaming newborn interrupting their sausage sizzle.

Becoming a mum and having a baby that never slept meant guilt hovered next to me like an annoying drone, following me everywhere, buzzing just out of sight. I spent the first few years feeling like everything I did wasn't good enough.

Maybe I shouldn't trust my gut, maybe scary Jenny and Mum were right. Should I give him a spoonful of Little Coughs cough syrup and let him sleep in a drawer?

Whenever anyone saw me in those early days, pumpkin mash stains down my top, trousers on backwards, I could see in their squinty expressions they thought I wanted help. Holding a baby is a green light, an invitation for unwanted opinion. A 'what worked for me' field day. There were so many ideas and tips that made no sense. Words drifted in one ear and out the other. As pointless as giving directions.

I avoided uninvited views by seeking out places where no one could find me. Basically, I did a runner. I found peace in multi-storey carparks, secluded benches in deserted playgrounds, and I sat on public toilets with the door locked for longer than I needed to. It was the only way I escaped the onslaught of judgement. I spent many afternoons walking around Aldi. I shoved the baby in a sling and wandered the aisles squeezing avocados and inspecting packets of sea salt cheese straws. I bought a jar of gherkins and a violin with its own carry case from the Special Buys section one afternoon, just because the security guard was getting suspicious.

'Do you play the violin?' asked the checkout lady.

Beep.

'No, not really.'

Beep.

'You shouldn't let that baby sleep in a sling. I just saw an article about the dangers of those.'

Beep.

For fuck's sake.

Beep.

'That's sixty-five dollars forty please. Don't go getting overtired sweetheart, remember …'

I know what she's going to say before it lands.

'You must sleep when the baby sleeps.'

Beep.

I nearly shoved the money down her throat, the perspex wall between us saving her. Apart from being told eating pasta and having reflux will result in a hairy baby, 'You must sleep when the baby sleeps' was the most annoying piece of advice anyone could give me. Not only did everyone say it all the fucking time, it was also as pointless as trying to find a fart in a hurricane.

I could not sleep in the day. Becoming a mother had not turned me into an owl. (Although having eyes in the back of my head when they became toddlers would have been useful.) Trying to sleep in the day was a slow form of torture. I might as well have been strapped to one of those medieval racks that stretched your body, that was how excruciating it was for me. I'd lie there, worrying about how tired I was. Every memory, failure, regret and worry floated into my head, with the sun beaming in, penetrating my soul through a gap in the curtains. I wondered if the baby was okay, if the washing was on, did I take the bins out, why did East 17 break up, and what was the dog in *Neighbours* called? I sat up in bed googling *Famous Labradors* when I should have been resting.

The checkout lady's comment was a sign that my 'time outs' in supermarkets were over. I couldn't even buy the weekly shop without someone telling me I'm failing.

Attempts at sleep routines worked for a few days, then broke down as quickly as an old car. I was so tired I no longer knew my own name. It was then we had to introduce the dreaded 'let them cry it out' method (suggested either by a smug child-rearing manual or an interfering busybody at a bus stop).

My husband sat next to the nursery door all night as we left George to cry until he couldn't anymore ... and fell asleep. It was traumatic. For me more than George. I went into my bedroom and bent a pillow around my head, covering my ears. Leaving a baby to cry wasn't in my character. I'm not sure it's in any mother's. But it worked, for a bit.

Nowadays, both the 'crying out' method and pretending my children are hamsters are no longer an option, I have to find some new tricks up my pyjama sleeve.

*

Fred has showered. Time for teeth.

'Right my darling little whipper-snapper, can you please go and brush your toothies,' I say in a very jolly Mary Poppins tone.

'No, I brushed my teeth yesterday.' Fred stomps as he says it.

'You must brush your teeth twice a day, Fred. We've talked about this.'

'No.'

My own teeth clench together, I push my nails into my palm.

Don't shout, Vic.

I swallow and glance at the fridge. The values glare back.

'How about, if you brush your teeth, I will tuck you in like a carrot and tell you your favourite story about Clumsy Bill – the silliest man in the world.'

'Okay Mummy. That will be fun.'

One down.

Two to go.

Since I multiplied, and my children became a herd rather than that one lone, bleating deer, every single bedtime is a relentless marathon, a race of endurance and stamina. That mother of one had it easy. I want to go back in time and tell her, 'Stop worrying! This is the good bit. Enjoy it.'

It's Nell next. Time to tackle her never-ending bedtime 'to-do list'. Getting Nell to sleep requires more steps than assembling Ikea flat pack furniture.

I go back and forth to her bedroom with beakers of water, books and teddies. I fantasise about having smiling supporters, standing in the hallway, egging me on, handing out refreshing oranges at every pitstop, 'You can do it! One more story! You've got this!' But bedtime in my house isn't a jolly fun run, it's like being kicked in the fanny by an angry Irishman wearing steel-capped boots.

I've cuddled, kissed, tucked and sung. I've even done a Carpenters medley. Nell lies next to me, wide awake, not letting her eyelids win.

'Right, I'm going now. Dad will be in for a kiss in a minute. Please just close your eyes.'

'Your turn,' I say when I'm back in the lounge. I hand the bedtime baton to my husband, John.

'Wish me luck,' he says.

His tactic is to fall asleep with her. It usually works. He appears an hour later with scruffy hair and lines on his face.

'I think she's gon– uuuurghhhhh.' A yawn interrupts him. As he stretches his arms over his head, I see her, standing behind him, staring straight at me, clutching her fluffy bunny rabbit.

And so it continues. Back and forth. There is a monster, five more toilet visits, a wide-eyed 'I'm scared of the dark' meltdown, a 'Can I have a slice of bread and butter?', and then the irrational 'I don't think any of my friends at school like me anymore' chat. It's not true, it's just that her brain shut down three hours ago. The whole debacle takes so long and is so draining that it leads me to my only fathomable solution.

Bribery.

At 9 pm I'm waving a five-dollar note above my daughter's head. She is dancing beneath it wearing her unicorn night dress, trying to grab hold of it, hands snapping upwards like a Venus fly trap.

'I will give you the money if you promise to go straight to sleep,' I say in a threatening (non–Mary Poppins) manner.

I realise attempting to bribe my children with cash to go to bed is not high-quality parenting. I'm certain my delightful little insomniac will raise the stakes tomorrow night and ask me for a tenner to brush her teeth. But the truth is, some days I have nothing left to give.

Nothing but spare change and a poorly read bedtime story.

My daughter seizes the note, smirks and wanders off towards her bedroom, somehow no longer afraid of the monster loitering in her cupboard. I feel slightly guilty that I only got her to go to bed with a payoff.

'You'd better not let the lady at your mummy classes know that you pay your children to go to bed,' my husband quips. 'You might get a detention.'

I don't laugh. As far as I'm concerned, it's a result. Two kids are now snoring like a couple of congested walruses.

All I have left is George, still awake, desperately trying to keep his eyes open so he can stay up for a bit longer, just like he did as a baby.

'It's nearly nine-thirty, sweetie. You've got school tomorrow.'

He gets up and then lollops off towards his bedroom.

No excuses.

No hamster feeders.

No exchange of funds.

Our only transaction is a kiss.

Goodnight, Jim-Bob.

Just Go and Play on the Road

I place my new trainers near the front door, ready for the morning.

'I didn't know you had trainers.' My husband has seen me. 'The only time I've ever seen you in any sports gear was when you dressed up as John McEnroe for Steve's fortieth.'

He is right. Tighty-whities, scuffed Nikes, a sweat band, tennis racquet and lots of swearing. It was an excellent party but the only exercise I did was lifting my pint.

'I've joined a boot camp. It starts at five-forty-five am down near the surf club. It's part of my Better Mummy Mission. Working out releases good endorphins. It might stop me calling the children twats as much.'

I had read an online article in *Marie Claire* about exercise enhancing cognitive tasks, improving mood, increasing energy and motivation. I then listened to a *Huberman Lab* podcast on running and dopamine hits. The science behind the benefits of exercise piqued an interest, and fitness has recently jogged into my algorithm. On Instagram every post I scroll past are women lifting weights or muscly instructors sharing out-of-breath reels yelling quotes, 'Eat Clean, Train Dirty!' I notice Facebook friends too, sharing smiling selfies after hiking up mountains. WhatsApp photos of old work colleagues cycling across France. A text from an old mate asking to sponsor his half-marathon. Adverts for hot yoga, multi-functional pelvic-floor trainers and bargain gym deals are filling my feed.

Also, all the mums I know are fit. Up bright and early for a run before sunrise. I sit with my coffee, watching as they pass in black shorts, pushing prams, sweating. I do want to be more like that. I'm certain it will make me feel better about myself, mentally and physically. I've been lethargic and tired recently, huffing and puffing when going up stairs, not keeping up with the kids like I should. I've been ignoring it; I reason I don't have time to clean my own teeth, let alone join a bloody running club.

But the results from a recent diabetes test show that I am very much 'on the cusp' of being medicated.

'You need to control this with diet and exercise, Vic,' said the doctor. 'Let's do another glucose test in six months.' As I sat in his poky little office, I knew that my 'can't be arsed' frame of mind was potentially life-threatening.

After years of avoidance, I'm beginning to realise that getting fit will help me be a better mum, and maybe stave off some health battles later in life. I want to live a long time, see my little people get married and have kids of their own. I want to hold my grandchildren (and know what it's like to give them back when they cry). It's time to drop my comfy dressing gown to the floor and step into some spandex. I buy some leopard print shorts, dust off my sports bra and set my alarm. I change the tone from a gentle buzz to the sound of a foghorn.

When the alarm goes off at 5.15 am, it's dark, it's cold, it's 5.15 am. I lean over, swipe it off and go back to sleep, then feel guilty all day at being such a loser.

On day two, I do the same.

On day three, I get up, go to the toilet, and decide to go tomorrow.

On day four, I lie in bed with my eyes open, staring into darkness pretending I don't exist.

On day five, I decide to start on Monday.

Done. Week one complete, and the only thing that went running was my mind.

I eat badly all weekend in preparation for my big comeback. So, not only have I not done any exercise, but I've eaten more than the week before and am riddled with shame over failing at my fitness plan.

Perhaps I am not destined for fitness? After all, the only 'squat' I've achieved in the last twenty-five years was secretly living in a lady's garage in Byron Bay for three months in

2002. It's been so long since I last exercised that I think I've forgotten how to do it.

Many moons ago, in a galaxy far, far away (Belgium), I was a gymnast. A leotard-wearing, toe-pointing tumbler. Even though my body was more suited to shot-put or the caber toss, I held my own on the squishy gym floor. My strong calves propelled me higher than the other tiny waifs in the club. I won vault competitions, swung from bars, and could do perfect splits on the beam. I once did a flamboyant floor routine to Strauss's 'The Blue Danube' waltz in front of a whole auditorium of onlookers and got a cheer when I landed a perfect backflip.

I was a good rounders player too, a game like baseball. The fieldsmen would shout, 'Whacker' as I entered the box holding a bat. I could hit that little ball far beyond the blackberry bushes at the back of the school pitch. The other team had to crawl around thorny undergrowth as I casually strutted between the bases. I knew my opponents would never be able to get me out. I had never felt more superior than on the rounders pitch. It was the only time I felt popular at school. Of course, I realise now they were probably shouting 'Wanker'.

My parents were as equally unsupportive of my sporting career.

'Mum, can I go to ballet?'

'No, you won't be very good. You're not built for it, Victoria. You're too stubby.'

'How about karate on Tuesdays?'

'I have "Keep Fit" on Tuesdays. Just go and play on the road.'

So, I gave up. Started smoking Silk Cut cigarettes and swigging Scrumpy Jack Cider behind the science laboratory and watched other girls wearing knee-high socks and cute bunches bouncing around the basketball court. By fourteen, I was so distracted by rebellion that I was no longer interested in standing on a podium and getting a rosette or competing against anyone unless the chant from the spectators was 'down it, down it, down it'.

My sobriety could also have something to do with my newfound interest in getting sweaty. For twenty-five years I was what you might call a normal, socially acceptable, binge drinker. A party girl with no off switch. I thought alcohol was my best mate and I was so immersed in drinking culture that I never bothered to look beyond the next glass of wine. Then, I had kids, the lethal combination of hangovers and children caused massive anxiety and I had to get some therapy to quit. It's the best thing I have ever done, but since giving up booze, gaps have appeared in my life and it's crucial I fill those spaces with something productive, a pastime that's the total opposite of my pre-sobriety life. Preferably something that doesn't involve downing pints, dribbling on strangers, or any questionable life choices that require a next-day apology tour.

Also, I want to be a good role model. I don't want my kids to be like me. I want them to love themselves and their bodies so much, that they don't numb out life like I did. So, I can either sit on the couch eating chocolate-covered raisins and watching *Downton Abbey* forever, or I can get up and get moving. Show them that if Mummy can do it, then they can too.

Until now, my lack of interest in sport means my kids' own interest has been neglected a little too. I had always nudged the kids away from certain activities, worried they would be very good at something, which would destroy my social life even more than becoming sober.

I'm embarrassed to admit that I have purposefully made sure my kids are not amazing swimmers. Getting up at 4 am and driving them to the local pool is not something I'm prepared to do. I didn't quite go so far as to bind their legs together or put drawing pins in their rash vests – I just droned on and on about how awful it would be to get up that early, how cold it would be in winter, and how it was likely there would be someone in the team who was better at it than them, therefore making it a total waste of time. Mean? Yes. Necessary? Also yes.

I steered George and Fred away from rugby, worried a player would bash their heads too many times and they'd end up in a hospital bed with a neck brace thinking they were Princess Margaret. And I won't even talk about the skate parks. Let's just say that because of our local ramp all the nurses at the local A&E know my children by their first names. I'm not very happy about ocean activities either. Sharks, jellyfish, rips, killer cone shells, tight budgie smugglers and boring tête-à-têtes about wind direction are enough to put off even the most well travelled of British mothers. So, I limit their sports to one safe sport per child per week. They seem happy with that, and I get to keep a bit of my soul – and, most importantly, my lie-in.

On Sunday, before I go to sleep, I hop on the boot camp group chat knowing I need some accountability. My people-pleasing ways mean I can't let anyone down. Even if I've never met them.

I write:

Looking forward to meeting you all tomorrow!

A little red heart appears straight away.

I find my new trainers and place them near the door again.

It's on.

*

'Good morning!'

Through the darkness, I see a man with a shaved head smiling at me.

'Are you Vic?'

'Yes, hello, I'm sorry I didn't make it last week, sick kids,' I lie.

'No worries. I'm Scott. Any injuries I should know about?'

'Nope.'

'Then there is just one thing to remember about this class. It's all about me.'

It's the only time I have ever laughed before 6 am.

The class is fun. The women are all friendly, in their fifties and sixties, kids left home and getting fit for the same reasons as me. To last longer. There is banter, encouragement, belly laughs and far too many burpees. But I enjoy it.

'We all go for a swim and coffee after. Are you coming, Vic?'

I follow the ladies onto the beach, where they run towards the waves in sports bras and leggings. I put down my towel, hide my car keys in a fold and hurry after them. They each join their palms above their heads and dive into breaking waves while I stand and watch in waist-deep water, hoping not to be eaten by a great white.

After the swim we gather at the café and sit along wooden benches, holding mugs of hot coffee that warm up our cold hands. We chat about life, kids and, surprisingly, women who heat up their vaginas over crockpots. I know right away that these are my kind of people.

Over the next few weeks, I go to boot camp as often as possible and start to feel a little bit fitter. More 'elastic outfit worthy'. The early mornings and new friendships are giving my mental health a huge boost, too. So, I add a daily walk into my routine. Big, long beach walks on blustery days, headphones in, listening to true crime or self-help podcasts as my feet sink into the sand. These jaunts spike my dopamine. Exercise, I hate to say it, is making me happy, and I want more.

I join a boxing gym. I had done it at boot camp and really loved it. Scott, the instructor, recommended a gym not far away run by an Olympian. 'It's a hard class Vic, I think you'll nail it.' I buy some gloves and wraps and book myself in.

I realise Nat, the coach, is tough before I meet her. I walk up her steep driveway and the sign above the gym comes into focus: *This is not a bakery … I do not sugar coat anything!* My stomach turns. *Can a slightly porky, ex-party animal really do this?*

I think about turning around and pretending this silliness never happened, but she's seen me. Nat is standing by the door, arms folded. She's wearing a tracksuit and a little beanie. She's pretty, with a strong physique. She looks me up and down as if to say, 'Here we go, another blow-in.'

'Hello, I'm Victoria. I'm here for the boxing class. You must be Natalie,' I say in my jolly, posh English accent.

She points to the long drive.

'Go for a run. Three laps.' She's blunt, but I like her no-bullshit attitude. It's frighteningly real and … fearing her means I will keep going.

I run, up and down the long driveway. Panting, and feeling a little dizzy, I head into the small building next to Nat's house. There are weights on the floor, an exercise bike and rower in one corner and a full-size boxing ring in another. Championship belts are hung on the walls and gold trophies sit collecting dust on a wobbly shelf.

'Wraps on.'

I look around at the other fighters. Men with rippling muscled bodies pair up. One with gloves, the other holding pads. Fierce women with tight braids start to spar against one another in the ring and others pound heavy bags that hang from metal chains. Guttural grunts echo as punches fly. As I stand to the side and watch on, I wrap up my wrists and hands and slide on my gloves. The cacophony of sights and sounds makes me feel like a real boxer, prepping for a big fight. I join the line of people practising right hooks.

The class is tough. There are a few moments in which I start talking myself out of it.

You can't do it. You're not good enough. You're not like these women.

I go over to the weights area and try to reset. I down some water and for some reason feel like I might cry. I see Nat walking over and I wonder if she might tell me off for taking a break.

'You need to hate yourself more, Vic.'

'What?'

I'm floored by her comment. My mind reels. How on earth could hating myself be helpful right now?

'You need to really hate yourself!' she says again.

I'm not sure it's the best or most empowering advice I've ever had, but when I think about her words, between swigs of water, I get it. For me, everything has to get bad before it gets good. Get drunk before I get sober. Get sad before I get therapy, get fat before I get fit and ... perhaps, be a bit of a crap mum before I can be a great one.

So, I do what she says. I stand up, pull my gloves back on and channel any self-doubt into punches. I get my hate on. Round two.

When the class is done, I feel like I've achieved something beyond my capability. As I sit bewildered on the floor, unwinding my wrist straps, Nat comes over and whispers so only I can hear, 'Ya done good today, Vic.' Words weigh more when they are few.

*

My trainers wait by the door every day now. My body feels strong, and I've noticed that letting off all this pent-up frustration means I'm calmer with the kids and I'm nowhere near as out of breath when playing football in the garden. I've even started taking the kids to exercise with me. We power-walk down to the beach and chat about their day at school as the dog weaves between our feet.

I go to boxing when feeling good, bad, tired, overwhelmed, or just plain pissed off. I go even when I don't want to. I know it will make me feel better. Trying to grasp boxing techniques, foot placements, hip movements and timings allows the daily grind to drip off me onto the padded floor. I concentrate so hard on combining each move that I completely forget about my day. Boxing liberates this daggy-shorted, sore-footed, cleaning machine from mother into warrior.

And warriors make excellent mums.

The Pros and Cons of
Invisible Friends

I am standing at the washing line with tears rolling down my cheeks. I didn't go to boot camp or boxing. I'm tired. I'm having one of those particularly difficult mumming days.

'What's the point?' I say to my husband as he passes me damp socks to hang out. 'No one ever listens to me. Everyone just ignores me. I repeat myself a hundred times, again and again, over and over. I'm fed up with it. I've become invisible.'

'They're not listening to me either. What shall we do?'

'Pack two bags and move to Barbados?'

He hands me my knickers, the state of them represents me quite well. Going grey and a bit baggy.

'If it's any consolation, we have two special guest stars over for a play this afternoon.'

'Oh god. Nell's special friends. At least I won't be the only person in the house who doesn't feel seen!'

We both laugh, in a slightly strangled way.

*

I first meet 'Dave Number Two' when my daughter scratches her little brother in the shower. Fred sprints into the lounge in tears, dripping wet, with four red lines running from the back of his neck to the top of his bum crack. The mark looks like an elongated barcode with freckles of blood appearing along the stripes.

I storm into the bathroom. 'Nell, get out of the shower now. Your brother is crying. You've really hurt him.'

Head bowed, she unhooks a towel and wraps it around her body. Her hair is wet and dripping onto the tiles.

'Why did you scratch him?'

'Dave Number Two told me to do it.'

'Who?'

'Dave Number Two. My special friend.'

'Is that a friend at school?'

'No Mum, he's over there.'

She points to an empty space near the toilet.

'And that's Loola.' She gestures to a spot on the ground near the toilet brush.

'Loola is inside everything,' she says with big wide eyes.

'What do you mean she's inside everything?'

'I mean she's everywhere, Mum.'

Her disturbing glare shatters any hopes of stable teenage years.

42

I am not falling for it. I know Nell has not created imaginary friends because she is lonely or traumatised, or just slightly odd. She's done it so she has someone to blame every time she is naughty. But for now, I ignore her transferral of responsibility onto the empty space next to the toilet, and tell her to apologise to her brother and get dressed.

I decide not to ask what happened to Dave Number One.

Loola and Dave Number Two both make appearances sporadically over the following weeks. When a vase is knocked over, when the skirting board is painted with pink nail varnish, again when the taps are left running after 'washing Daddy's iPhone', and finally when Fred emerges from her bedroom with a *Dumb and Dumber* haircut.

Their names fall from her mouth without hesitation.

'Loola and Dave Number Two did it. They like being naughty!' she says as she hides the pair of scissors behind her back.

Part of me respects Nell's dedication to the cause and part of me thinks she's mad, but you see, there are pros and cons of having imaginary friends and I work out ways of using their almost existence to make my life a little easier.

*

After school, the kids all climb into the back seat. Bags are shoved in the footwell, seatbelts are pulled down and clicked in, and Nell's question comes before a hello.

'Mummy, can I have a playdate today?'

'I don't have time to organise a playdate now. You need to tell me the week before. I can't just invite someone round last minute.'

And then the thought enters my mind. I can use the invisible troublemakers to my advantage.

'You will just have to play with Dave Number Two and Loola today.'

I see her tense up.

She's not sure what to do.

If she tells me she made them up, she's then guilty of all her past indiscretions. I see her nose twitch as she considers her options.

'Okay Mum, I will just play with Loola and Dave Number Two today,' she answers with arms crossed high on her chest.

I look in my wing mirror at my eldest son, George. He is twirling his finger around in a small circle next to his ear gesticulating that, yes, he was right, his sister is insane.

I give him a little smile. He rolls his eyes then looks out the window.

*

I let Nell carry on with her pretend relationships because having the little see-through duo over for a playdate is much better than putting up with her other friend, Charlie. Nell met him at glee club. He's one of those kids who seems to have a constant line of slimy snot leaking from his nose onto his top lip, he answers back, thinks he knows everything, breaks Hot Wheels tracks, brags about money and throws food around the house like a farmer sowing seeds. I find myself being a bit short with Charlie when he visits. He's an old man in a child's body and he marches around my house like a moody landlord.

In comparison Dave Number Two and Loola are excellent house guests, respectful and polite. They don't piss on the toilet seat or steal all my raspberries from the fridge. They *don't* outstay their welcome or shout about getting a new expensive bike. You wouldn't even know they were there. The only downside is that I will have to pay for Nell to see a psychiatrist someday.

But today, after putting out the washing and a successful playdate with the dynamic indistinguishable duo, Charlie comes over. Nell loves him so occasionally I must give in. They make a mud pie and smear it all over the deck, pick all the herbs and re-plant them in a fairy garden (a flower pot full of rocks) and then Charlie predictably helps himself to all my raspberries. He denies it but the trails of red juice mixed in with his snot are a dead giveaway.

Charlie's mum arrives at 4:30 pm to pick him up. I'm hoping for nothing more than a beep and a head round the gate, a 'yoo-hoo' and a leave-the-car-running type of grab, but no such luck. The car is parked, the engine is off and she's coming in. All of a sudden being invisible is very appealing.

'Sorry I'm late, I had Pilates. How's my Charlie?'

'Yes, he's been fine.'

She plonks her bum up on a stool at the kitchen bench and begins to talk at me.

Very quickly, I know the name of her tennis partner's dog, what face cream she uses, and why she can't eat tomatoes. She goes on and on. This one-way conversation is enough to make my ears bleed. I sit opposite her and pretend to show interest in her life, which teacher her snub-nosed offspring had last year, where she bought her rattan pendant lights, what day care list she signed up to a year before Charlie even existed and lots of other boring rubbish. I nod and make inane comments like, 'Oh that's a great idea. Thirty-year fixed mortgages are the best.' And, 'Yes, wow, Boho Nation. Forty per cent off tropical placemats. Amazing.'

I am way too good at pretending to be interested in people I don't like. I ask questions, I smile in all the right places, I tell funny anecdotes and offer them a second lamington. I'm amiable. I show interest, I look like I care.

Feigning a level of interest in topics and people that bore me is a skill I perfected in my youth. At school, I shot my hand up every few minutes, so Miss Gittings thought I was a keen student. As soon as her back was turned, I wrote notes to boys on ripped out pages of *The Canterbury Tales* and sold cigarettes for ten pence each to Fighty Katie, who sat behind me. When my mum pontificated about my 'attitude' as a teen I nodded as if I was taking in her wise lessons, but fantasised her head would fall off mid-sentence. During a lecture at uni (the only one I went to the entire time I was there), I looked like I was scribbling intellectual notes about 'revenue performance management' when, really, I was carving my name alongside a cock and balls into the desk with a small pen knife.

I look at my watch. My tea is tepid and Charlie's mum, dressed in full Lorna Jane, ponytail high, perfect tanned midriff on display, drones on about growing up in Victoria. Her chatter seeps into dinner-prep time and even though I am as bored as a teenager without an internet connection, I find myself nodding along, giving her the impression we are going to be lifelong buddies.

'… and I've just gone vegan. I'm feeling amazing. You should do it too, Vic.'

'That sounds great,' I say. I don't mention my brief stab at going vegan. I didn't last long. I went to a pub quiz and won the raffle. A meat tray. A week that started out with me saving pigs from the slaughterhouse ended in a bacon sandwich.

'I have time for another tea. Do you have chai?' she asks. I want to say, 'Haven't you got better things to do than sit here and waffle on at me about crispy tofu slabs with peanut sauce and cabbage slaw?' But instead I say, through gritted teeth, 'I have masala,' and stick the kettle on.

Charlie's mum, it seems, has all the time in the world. She has one child. She has one portion of spag bol to cook. One load of washing. One lot of homework to help with and one bedtime story.

Raising multiple kids is very different from raising one, I realise two shags too late. Having one kid is the equivalent of having a slow cooker. You put everything into them and whatever comes out is perfect. You can't go wrong. Three is like having several cooking pots on the stove, one boiling over, one getting burnt on the bottom and the other simmering, waiting to explode.

She's still talking …

'… and then another mum asked if I would join her walking group, and guess what, we're going to do a sponsored trek in Nepal …'

'Righto, I'd better get on,' I say hoping to end the monotony and sort out dinner for my three bubbling pots.

At last, my obvious hint jolts her motherly instinct.

'Is it that time already? Gosh, this was lovely, Vic. We should do this again, are you around this time next week?'

'I'm so sorry, I'm busy next week. I have two very good friends coming over … Loola and Dave Number Two.'

A Bit Woo Woo

March

'Are you okay?'

'What do you mean, "Am I okay?"'

My podcast co-host, Hamish, looks concerned. His eyes scan the room.

'I mean, are you okay? Mentally?'

'I think so?' I say wondering what he is poking at.

I follow his eye line.

The small recording studio (AKA Fred's bedroom) is a mess. A piss-stained mattress leans up against the window frame, drying out after a Fred-related accident; a rotting tangerine festers next to Hamish's mic stand; clothes are strewn across the floor; and there's a certain smell. My dog Sandy's grassy vomit from the week before still lingers like sour milk.

I realise this is indeed an 'Are you okay?' kind of moment.

'Oh god, sorry Hamish. It's a mess in here. It's so hard to work, clean, parent and everything else. I'm falling behind and I can't seem to catch up.'

'Well … maybe you should come with me to my breathwork class this weekend. It might help you put things in perspective and help you deal with parenting a bit better.'

I like him, so I decide not to punch him in the face when he suggests this.

'You know I'm not into all that stuff, Hame.'

He is right though; I need to do something. My Sunny Days Parenting tips have faded away as life got too busy. I've missed a few classes, my notes are in the footwell of the passenger seat in my car, trampled with mud, and no matter how many de-stress parenting apps I download or walks I go on, I still feel like my shoulders are up round my ears.

I don't want to feel highly strung. I want to feel calm and happy. I want to learn how to be off my tits on life, without any liquor pulsing through my veins. So, I'm going to give in, delve into more-alternative ways to stop me being a shouty mum. Not extreme woo. No aura cleansing, Om tattoos or chakra balancing, just a peek into what lies beneath my pessimism. It's time to throw my preconceived ideas into the metaphorical singing bowl.

*

I've tried getting all transcendental 'n' shit a few times in my life, but it's never really worked out. When I lived in Manly, in Sydney's north, I went through a stage of trying to fit in with all the hippie, spiritual mums. I did a tantric yoga class where I lay on the floor on my back for an hour as women made guttural orgasmic sounds all around me. A man with a well-groomed beard and long robe wandered around the room, occasionally kneeling and whispering into the ears of the moaning ladies. It was awkward, to say the least. Before I could feel his hot breath in my earhole, I got up and left, questioning if it wasn't just a beard he was grooming.

I tried Reiki, but the only energy that channelled through me was the bad breath of the so-called 'Master'. Every time she exhaled it was like the bin truck went past. I ended up trying to hold my breath for an hour. Not very comforting or therapeutic at all.

I did a sound healing session during which I fell asleep. Then I had acupuncture when I was trying for a second baby (a pain in the arse that cost nearly as much as raising a child for eighteen years) and I've had lots of massages. The waft of scented candles, soft panpipe music and dimmed lighting lead me to believe I am about to have a relaxing, tranquil experience. I never learn. As I lie facedown, with my head in the hole, my nose runs and drips onto the floor and I don't know where to put my hands. I end up letting them fall down towards the ground and all the blood rushes to my fingertips. And there I stay. Arms about to drop off, telling an aggressive, dry-handed stranger that what he is doing to me doesn't hurt, when really it does.

I even tried an ecstatic dance class in the hope of feeling a bit more grounded and earth mother-y. My sister, Louise, had been to a class and loved it. I then saw a poster about a class pinned to the cork board outside my local shop. It was a sign. (It literally was.) It showed a picture of a women with feathers in her hair, arms outstretched towards the sky. Underneath, it said, 'Release yourself to rhythm – allow blissful beats to take you into a trance-like state and feeling of ecstasy.' So, I went. What the sign should have said was, 'Stand self-consciously in a room full of people you don't know while one woman, who's *really* into it, prances around the room waving her arms like an agitated swan.'

I once visited Lumbini in Nepal, (the rumoured) birthplace of the Buddha. It was a *very* spiritual place. Colourful prayer flags flapped in rows near a white fort with a red, tiled roof. A line of young monks in orange robes sat in silence on steps that led to a small lake. I heard the creak of ancient prayer wheels turning and the beat of a drum somewhere in the distance.

People were queuing outside a low-set building with flaking white paint. Each of them sliding a big toe down their heel to remove sandals as they entered. I followed suit and stepped onto the wooden boardwalk that led me to the ruins where Emperor Ashoka had built a brick temple around the actual spot where the Buddha was believed to be born. Visitors ahead of me dropped to their knees as they reached this historical, holy destination. They all looked bewildered, shocked that they had reached the end of their pilgrimage. As I watched on, various irrational thoughts flooded my mind:

Should I drop to my knees? What would I say? Would people be offended if I wave? I couldn't just give a thumbs up and then walk on ... Could I?

I hung back for a second while unravelling my divine dilemma and got a little shove from a tiny lady in a red sari behind me.

'You go now.'

I knelt.

Then mumbled ... the 'Wham Rap!'

I opened an eye and saw the lady looking at me. I wondered if she was a George Michael fan, but decided it was not a good time to ask. I closed my eyes and recited the next verse.

As far as anyone knew, I was praying and being all holy. When I finished, I stood up and tapped my body.

'Testicles, spectacles, wallet and watch,' I said as I moved my hand around my body, mapping out a Christian cross.

The lady in the red sari nodded at me, seemingly convinced by my act. I joined my hands in prayer position, stuck a calm, otherworldly expression on my face, and shuffled backwards while bowing at her. It was very silly. I sighed with relief and went outside. I walked slowly around the gardens, looking all peaceful and serene, and came upon a door with a big sign hung above it: *Meditation rooms.*

I remember thinking as I stood there, *Well, it's now or never.*

I needed a bit of awakening, especially after sleeping in that hostel bunk with nothing but an itchy yak-wool blanket to keep me warm, and perhaps, after a dedicated hour-long meditation session, I'd be ready to become more spiritual or at least understand myself a bit better.

I stepped in. The tiled floor felt cold on my bare feet and a wind blew through open arches in the thick stone walls. A chill snuck up my trouser leg. A few people sat cross-legged, facing a statue at the front. I went to join them, but was pulled backwards by someone tugging my T-shirt.

'Go no further,' said a voice with a German accent.

I turned and was met nose to nose by a man with a scrunched-up face.

'Have you booked the meditation for this day?'

'No, I just thought I'd pop in and give it a try. Is that okay?'

'This is not a drop-in for travellers. You must leave. Now.'

He manually turned me around using my shoulders, like he was preparing me to stick a tail on a donkey, and pushed me from the room.

So much for finding myself and my divine goddess within. All I found was a windy gusset and an angry German.

I went back to the hostel and packed my backpack, which was much lighter having replaced *The Miracle of Mindfulness* and *The Life of Buddha* with a ragged copy of *Hello! Magazine*.

*

With my lack of faith unscathed, I carried on disbelieving and being a terrible sinner for about another fifteen years.

Then on my birthday last year, Hamish nudged me, unwittingly, towards another more unconventional therapy. He invited me over to his house under the lure of a slice of cake and had an inflatable ice bath waiting for me. 'Surprise!'

I stripped off and hopped in without hesitation. In the grand spectrum of self-improvement, an ice bath didn't feel extreme. I shivered through three whole minutes, breathing slowly and praying my toes didn't fall off, then climbed out, frozen but buzzing. I felt amazing for the rest of the day – and, of course, got the all-important "Look at me, I'm lowering myself into an ice bath!" Instagram post.

But now, sitting in Fred's messy room, feeling overwhelmed, I know it's time to try something new. I have nothing to lose. Maybe Hamish's breathwork class is what I need to do.

I turn to the keyboard and type *breathwork* into Google.

Breathwork is a method of breath control that attempts to give rise to altered states of consciousness, and to have a positive effect on physical and mental wellbeing.

An altered state of consciousness sounds very appealing. Anything positive happening to my physical and mental wellbeing is better than throwing brooms at walls and witnessing my own mental undoing.

Hamish is an all-round good chap, so I decided to trust him.

'All right Hamish, I'll go, but don't expect me to be happy about it.'

Later that week, Hamish is excited as we drive down the motorway towards my enlightenment. He chats all the way. But after a night of no sleep owing to a weird animal making grunting noises outside my bedroom window and three uninvited bodies thrashing around next to me like the possessed, I am not in the mood.

I am not okay.

But I decide to follow Hamish's lead. Go in there full of joy and positivity, and hope life will be richer after the experience. I am a hundred dollars down, so they have work to do. We pull up at a very ordinary house. No sign of woo. Hamish rings the doorbell and the door is opened by a very handsome smiling man.

'Hi, I'm Yannick, I'm your guide.'

When he says 'guide', I swallow back the little bit of sick that pops up to say, 'Namaste.'

He leads us to an open-plan lounge with yoga mats rolled out and folded blankets on each end. There is a Buddha statue in the corner, a pot of cacao bubbling on the stove, and the smell of sandalwood drifts over from a little incense stand on the mantelpiece.

A few people nod at me. A lady dressed in jean shorts and a hoodie comes over to take my hands into hers and asks, 'Are you ready?'

It's a good question. The truth is, no, I am not. I'm feeling self-aware and over-exposed. I'm not sure what is going to happen but already it feels emotionally confronting. I'm not even very good at opening up to my husband. I don't go deeper than the weather forecast or what episode of *Britain's Got Talent* we're on, let alone release all my inner feelings to a group full of people I have never met before.

'Not really, I'm not really into all this,' I say.

'Don't worry. Just go with it.'

So ... I went.

I spend the next hour and a half lying on the ground, blanket up to my chin, eye mask blocking out the light, following Yannick's commands.

I breathe to the rhythm of a loud drum. In and out. In and out.

Nothing is happening. I hear someone laughing, someone crying, another moaning. I try to relax a little and let go of my preconceived ideas and ego. I want to feel whatever they are feeling.

I sense someone is next to me. Warm breath in my ear.

'I'm going to turn your hands over now, Vic.'

My hands are on the floor facing down. Whoever is whispering to me moves around my body and gently turns them over. Within a second of this small change in position it feels as if the clouds part in my brain. Emotions fill my heart, tears leak from my eyes, and a strong column of light shoots from my hands up into the sky. I have no idea what is going on. Images of my beautiful children swamp my mind – running on the beach, asking me to play a game and me … saying, 'Not now.'

My work is getting in the way of us.

They need me and I'm too distracted.

The words tap into my soul.

The drumbeats are louder now, my body shakes as I see my life from above. It is clear what I am doing wrong and as the beat decelerates, something shifts.

'In your own time, open your eyes and then join us in the kitchen for the cacao ceremony.'

I look over at Hamish. He is smiling at me.

I smile back and give him a thumbs up.

We sit in a circle afterwards, sip spicy cacao and chat about our experience. I admit in front of the whole room, 'I thought you were all woo woo weirdos at first, but I really enjoyed it.' My honesty gets a guffaw and Yannick abruptly moves his gaze to the person next to me.

Afterwards, in the car on the way home, I feel high. My anxiety seems to have lifted and I feel a bit lighter. Whatever happened at that house, be it spiritual or the fact that hyperventilating on a stranger's living room floor has opened a part of my brain that even Indiana Jones couldn't dig up, it doesn't really matter. What does matter is that I feel much clearer about what I have to do.

'I think I need to be more conscious of my work time, phone time and home time. I've been prioritising my work over my kids,' I say to Hamish.

As the words come out, I know I have evolved in some way. It's not seismic, but it's profound. This acknowledgement of my mistakes makes my skin tingle. I've somehow unearthed answers to questions I didn't know I had. Maybe I am a bit woo woo after all?

'Thanks for today, Hamish. I feel ... better. And I am going to clean up the dog sick properly when I get home.'

He laughs.

'That's very spiritual of you, Vic!'

The Sneeze

The breathwork session got me thinking. When exactly did I start to rank work over children? Was this just a trait of a busy mum? Or was I neglecting some of my homely responsibilities to feel a bit of freedom from motherhood? I sat in my office the following morning and tried to pinpoint where I was slacking. I made a list of some of the events I had missed.

A trumpet recital. A dance performance. A school assembly, in which Nell performed 'I'd Like to Teach the World to Sing' using sign language. It had taken her weeks to learn.

'You are coming, aren't you?'

'I've got a meeting, Nellie, I can't come to everything.' I stare at the toaster unable to confront her disappointed expression.

There have been other times too. An hour after I was supposed to be at the Mother's Day pampering in Fred's classroom, I get a text from a mate: *Where are you? It's nearly finished!* I ditch a Zoom call and get there for the make-up session in which my face is held down and someone's dead mother's mascara is dragged over my eyelashes.

'Where were you, Mummy?'

I missed the email about Grandparents' Day at Fred's Kindy last year too.

'Tilly said my granny didn't come because she's dead.'

'She's not dead, sweetie. She's just old.'

'Same thing.'

Once, I left George waiting outside the school hall after *Frozen* rehearsals because, if I'm honest for a moment, I forgot he existed.

Then there was the sneeze.

I heard a big 'Ahhhhhhhhchooooooooooooooo'. I thought nothing of it and carried on tapping my keyboard, then a little head poked around the door.

'Don't worry, Mum, I blessed myself.'

Guilt hung from me like heavy bags of shopping.

'Mummy, do you love your laptop more than me?'

'No of course not, Nell. I just have work to do.'

'Can we play with my dolls for a bit?'

'Not right now.'

I reached out and touched her cheek. She was the prettiest thing I'd ever seen. I knew I should play with her, but I didn't. I turned back to my screen and carried on.

I realised I rated work higher than my own daughter.

Success, in the workplace, has come at an odd time for me. A time when, according to archaic societal customs, I should be a stay-at-home mum, worrying about mould in the shower and an overflowing tea towel drawer. But for the first time in my life, I am achieving and pursuing a career, so, I have *two* full-time jobs.

1. Parenting
2. What I really want to be doing

Trying to do everything means I am not very good at doing anything, and the principal occupation of in-house 'CEO' (Child Evolution Officer) suffers. Not only do I miss events, I rush dinners, I don't have time to change the beds and I forget about charity bake sales. At a recent fundraising stall, all I managed to raise was a few eyebrows from the apron-clad bread bun mums when they saw my tray of shop-bought oat slices.

Mumming is just another job, in a long line, that I am rubbish at. If parenting had a boss, I would have been sacked by now for 'underperforming' in my role. The only 'blue sky thinking' I've ever done was look out of a plane window for eight hours after taking too much Valium on a flight to Bangkok in 1997.

I'm not someone who has ever really had any goals.

When the teacher asked at school, 'What career would

you like?' I remember other kids shooting up their hands and saying, 'Doctor', 'Teacher', 'Vet' and 'Hairdresser'.

'What about you, Victoria?' the teacher asked me.

'I want to be one of the ladies in the windows.'

'A window dresser. That would be a lovely job.'

'No, one of the ladies that wears a feather boa, lacy bra and sits there all day smoking.'

The teacher moved on.

We were living in Belgium at the time. Dad's job took us there for three years. Whenever friends from England came to visit us, on the way back from the airport, Dad would do a detour of the red-light district. Both my parents and their friends seemed to find this mini sightseeing tour quite amusing. As Dad kerb-crawled, I waved at the nice ladies from the back seat.

'Look Mum, she's waving back!'

I had no idea why they sat on high stools with red light bulbs dangling over their heads. I never thought to ask. I was only seven, too young to know that being a sex worker in a Brussels brothel wasn't an addition to my curriculum vitae my teacher would approve of.

*

I got my first 'proper' job at sixteen, working in Michael Caine's restaurant as a kitchen porter. I washed pots, oven trays and cutlery. I cleared plates and stole cumquats off half-eaten cheesecakes and popped them in my mouth when the head chef wasn't looking. It was the highlight of my shifts. When I wasn't loading the industrial dishwashers, being the youngest and female meant I was given all the shitty jobs. I pulled backbones out of stinking, floppy squid, peeled potatoes and mopped floors. If the sous-chef was bored, he lifted me up and hung me on a meat hook by the back of my apron and left me there to dangle like a duffle coat while the rest of the staff pointed and laughed. I chuckled along with them. I had heard a rumour that the head chef stabbed someone once, so I would play along until one of the servers helped me down.

When I travelled in Australia in my early twenties, I did whatever I could to get to my next destination. I worked in an office in Sydney's CBD, and a deli in Bondi. (I was sacked after the boss found me hungover, retching into a drain when I should have been slicing prosciutto.) I laid tables (and the Spanish barman) at a seaside café in Airlie Beach and spent a few weird months living in a tent on a cherry farm just outside Melbourne.

On the first day, I opted to work in the sorting factory, separating 'good cherry' from 'bad cherry'. It was as mind-numbing as it sounds. On the second day, I went picking in the orchard. I climbed ladders and twisted stalks until the barrel hanging from the leather straps slung over my shoulders cut into my skin. The only break was a visit to the onsite portaloo where giant huntsman spiders decorated plastic walls. Everyone seemed much quicker at the job than me, filling five barrels to my measly one. It was only after stumbling across my co-workers' accommodation at the back of the farm that I discovered them with sleeves rolled up, injecting speed into their forearms.

'Fancy a hit, Vic?'

I was shocked but I tried to play it cool.

'No thanks. I'm not very good with injections.'

I decided it was wise to come back from travelling with a couple of scruffy Lonely Planets and a tattoo instead of a methamphetamine addiction. I left the farm the next day.

There were a couple of stints of trying to unpack the backpack and move home to join the rat race. I was an estate agent in London for a year. I bought a second-hand suit at Oxfam and pretended to care about house prices and gas certificates.

I worked as a travel agent, booking trains, planes and hostels for other people instead. The company once ran a competition. 'Whoever can sell the most Air France tickets in the office will win two return flights to anywhere in the world!' I told every single customer who wanted a weekend in Paris that the Eurostar train had 'work on the tracks' that particular day and they would have to fly. I spent three weeks in Cuba, where I danced salsa until dawn on the cobbled streets of Havana.

I often lost jobs because I was hungover a lot back then. So, the only way I was ever going to have a career, beside my drinking one, was to work for myself. Self-employment meant I had no one to disappoint and couldn't be sacked if I pulled a sickie.

I imported silver jewellery from Thailand to sell at market stalls. I would wake up when it was dark and drive down silent motorways to towns and villages where I set up tables and laid out necklaces on silky cloth. I did it for fifteen years, during two pregnancies and after. It didn't affect the normal demands of being a mum. I was able to balance my job and kids without feeling like anyone was missing out. I was lucky, I had a husband who had a good job as a window cleaner, and his flexible schedule meant he could pick up the kids from school or take them to sports when I was at a market. It was a role that paid off, it gave me the time and space to be a good mum.

Then, I got sober. A brain that had sat dormant for twenty-five years kicked into action. I started writing and podcasting and ditched working at the markets. I had found my passion and purpose. My lack of career before meant I was going to give it everything now. I stirred bolognaise with one hand and tapped at my laptop with the other. I took calls as I breastfed and did interviews while pushing swings at the park. I told my story until I felt heard. For the first time in my life I was thriving, and I've tried to maintain a bridge between my work and my kids, but now, as I get busier, the current is getting too strong and I am getting sucked under.

'Just let me finish this. I promise I will do craft with you tomorrow night.'

'Please, go away, Nellie. Mummy needs time to get this done.'

'Can you just leave me alone for five more minutes?'

I rush through some editing, schedule a post for socials and when I'm done, I look over at the kids. Three heads in a row watching TV. They're quiet and happy. I send a final email, fold my laptop closed and take a moment to unpack their school bags. I find a squashed banana in George's, a pair of wet shorts in Fred's, and some drawings in Nell's. I stealthily place the papers in the rubbish bin without making a sound. As I close the lid, I look down to see the painting on top. It's of us, with a big heart hovering above. We're holding hands and have huge smiles. Underneath, in her funny chook scratch handwriting it says: *My mummy is the best mummy in the holed wide werld.* It's so uncomplicated. So perfect.

I know then that I need to make more time. Organise my days better and be more present with my kids. I make a mental note to switch off my laptop at 2 pm every day and not look at it again.

I peel the drawing from the pile and stick it on the fridge.

'Bless you, Nell.'

Death Metal with a Crow

It's time for the next phase of the mummy overhaul. A 'before' and 'after' shot of life. If I want to get better at this parenting malarkey I must start choosing them over work. Which means I have to show up, get organised and ... do stuff I absolutely hate.

The problem is that I hate many, many things. I hate those stupid ribbon loops to keep clothes on their hangers. Queues at water parks. People who lick their lips too much. The way my mum burps out of the corner of her mouth. Death metal. Porridge overflowing in the microwave. Used tea bags in the sink. Playing Scrabble with my husband. Birds. Mostly crows. Marzipan. Opera. Running. Quicksand. Overripe bananas. Underripe bananas. Dry ski slopes. People who purposefully take ages when I'm waiting for their parking space. Wet swimming costumes. Cold shoulders. High heels. Turkish delight. Canned laughter. People who say 'pacifically' instead of 'specifically'. Passwords. Toe socks.

The noise plane toilets make when you flush. Getting out of bed when it's dark. Oh, and there are also lots of things I hate about being a mum.

When the kids were little, I hated potty training. I held back on starting until the hotter summer months; that way I could just let them roam around naked to pee in plant pots. They also did bush wees, shower wees, dog bowl wees, pool wees and the occasional all-over-the-toilet wee. It was easier to let them loose and hope they peed in suitable places because actual potty training required organisation, something I've never been very good at.

'Wild wees' worked at home, but when we went out in public I needed to be prepared. I had to pack spare underpants and trousers for the trainee and for me because often, both of us got a soaking. I'd be out enjoying a nice chat with a mummy mate when a warmth spread over me. It felt quite nice until I realised what it was.

My children were very subtle when it came to toileting. I could never predict what was around the S-bend. Facial expressions and posture didn't falter when there was an incoming potty event. I had seen other kids go red, grab their crotches and run in circles when they needed to go, but not my little psychos – they were utterly nonchalant. Faces docile and unsmiling as dark patches appeared on bottoms. It was almost like they just did it to watch *me* go red and run around in circles.

'Quick! Don't worry, Nell. It's just an accident. Wipes! You must try and let Mummy know so we can go to the bathroom.' I shoved soaked clothes in a small plastic bag and tied a knot in the top and then forgot they were there until I found the bag a week later, pierced a hole in it and got a waft worse than a dead badger's fanny.

Luckily, as a family we have only had two major poopy incidents in the past twelve years. One was the 'diarrhoea squirt' in the car seat. It shot up the back of the babygrow, out of the collar and onto the neck rest. (That clean-up is a parenting must. In the child-rearing Olympics it would be the third event after the bolognaise puke in the top bunk bed, and the untangling of a slinky.) The only other major poo party was when my husband threw Fred in the air and a solid baby turd tumbled out of the side of a loose nappy. It was like a falling meteor. Before my husband considered his action, his hand reached out and snatched the pellet plop, then the baby, from the sky.

I am so glad that all my kids no longer piss their pants or shit themselves. I've had enough of dealing with nappies and waste from other people's orifices. (Although I do plan on exacting my revenge when I'm eighty-five.)

Poo aside, as part of my new 'trying to be a better mommy' (say it in an American accent, please) approach, I decide to do a few things I hate. So I put on a pair of high heels and eat marzipan while listening to death metal with a crow. Not really! Instead, against my better judgement, I bake scones wearing a plastic apron. When I arrive at school pick-up, I have a little bit of flour on my face that I put there on purpose. I hope someone will notice and think how fucking amazing I am.

'Yes, scones,' I'll say with a smarmy expression. 'I try and bake for the children at least once a week.' I won't mention the inedible lumps of coal dumped into the bin. I will tell half the story in order to appear at least half the mother people imagine me to be.

Later that week, I do yet another hateful task. I turn up to school assembly. George is getting an award for being kind in class. I can't stand going to assembly because instead of just enjoying it and singing along to the national anthem, I use it as an opportunity to convince people to like me. I arrive early and sidle up to the headmaster, who I am desperately trying to befriend. I lead a one-way conversation about the time I got my big toe stuck in a trampoline as a child and, because he makes me nervous, I laugh at the end even though it isn't funny. He walks away with his head bowed and I'm left feeling like an idiot.

As I make my way towards the seats, I wave at other mums I know like I'm on the red carpet. 'Yoo-hoo.' 'Love the outfit.' I act extrovert when inside ... I am questioning myself. I sit in the front row and clap much louder than everyone else because I obviously love my child the most.

I even shout, 'Love you, George' when he takes to the stage. It's embarrassing; but I can't help getting swept up in the excitement. I leave feeling self-conscious knowing I've made a dick of myself, yet sort of pleased that I have been socially awkward for the sake of my offspring. School assemblies, for some reason, are a very emotionally confusing event.

Overall, I've had one of those weeks where everything goes well. I've not shouted (as much), the Sunny Days 3-2-1 countdown method is healing my vocal cords and the kids get ready on time. There is even a 'Thanks for dinner, Mummy!'

'I really appreciate you saying that, Fred,' I whimper from the spot on the floor where I have collapsed in total shock.

When life is going well, I'm lured into a false sense of security. The kids' jolliness seeps into my every pore and, before I know it, I find myself planning a day of activities that are outside my parenting comfort zone.

Round one: I set up an amateur pottery station on the dinner table. Cutters, rollers, little letter printing blocks and a slab of clay. I pull off a lump of clay and place it on a round mat for each of them. They all sit.

'It feels funny, Mummy.'

'Yeah, I don't like it. It's slimy.'

It takes thirty minutes to set up for three minutes of play and then another thirty minutes to clean up. Deep breath.

Round two: I build a car out of a cardboard box and run down our road wearing it while they all point and laugh at me. Then they all sit making their own one. The stabbing of scissors through thick cardboard makes me slightly on edge but, overall, this activity is a success. We all race down the road making revving noises and crashing into one another until the cars fall apart.

Round three: I place pizza bases and little bowls filled with ingredients out on the kitchen bench and we make pizza faces for dinner. This one also goes surprisingly well and, even though the salami noses look like wonky penises, they taste yummy. I have successfully set the pessimist free and, for this one perfect day, I parent like a trooper.

My children have spidey senses when I am like this. They can feel I have softened a little and am more pliable than a pot of playdough.

'Muuuum? Can we go camping this weekend?'

Oh god.

I hate camping. I hate everything about it. Camping for me is a slow form of torture. I'd rather be poked in the eye with a spike for an hour than sleep in a glorified plastic bag. I hate shuffling to the bathrooms in a manky robe, carrying slippery bottles of shampoo and wet soap in a bag. I hate strangers' hair in shower plugs. I hate blow-up beds that fire me into the sky like a human cannonball when my husband lies down. I hate shouting, 'Car!' every five minutes, so my oblivious children don't get run over. I hate the animals: mozzies, snakes, rodents, spiders and wombats sniffing around. I hate cooking utensils that are joined together. I hate people in fishing shirts. I hate plastic washing-up bowls. I hate being cold at night and hot in the morning. I hate beef sausages. I hate sand in my sleeping bag and bum crack. I hate the sound of zips. I hate it all.

Instead of kicking back and soaking up mother nature, I expect to spend our camping weekend running around like a lunatic checking that my children haven't stepped on smouldering embers of a campfire, burnt their fingers on a sparkler or been accosted by a weirdo in the toilets.

The face of the nice lady from Sunny Days Parenting burns a hole in the back of my eyelids and her words fill my head.

Try doing some activities they will enjoy, that will build trust and heal your fractured relationships.

Damn you, conscience! I begrudgingly book a campsite within a five-kilometre radius of the house. I decide to do something I hate for the kids, like I do everything for the kids. For them, I will get my pinky finger caught in a foldout table, drink tea out of a metal cup and sit on a recently used, warm toilet seat. That afternoon I wander the half-empty shelves of Kmart searching for a small gas stove and marshmallows.

I didn't always hate camping. As a child I loved it. My aversion towards it only started after having children. Before kids, camping felt like an adventure – a journey of self-discovery among tall trees, sand dunes and bearded nomads. I was quite happy to go for a slash in the woods and eat beans from a tin can. I was freer, more independent. But camping with children is a whole new ball game.

The shouting match starts before we've even left home. As we pack, there are fights over the colour of fishing nets ('No! *I* want the pink one') and teddies ('Can Tiger *and* Rabby come, Mum?') and then a punching game to decide who sleeps in the single blow-up bed and who gets the double. It results in Fred having a scratched, bleeding arm. 'I told you it would end in tears.' I give him a cuddle and a band-aid. Then I try to pack the Eskie with the kids still running around at my feet, being no help whatsoever.

'Can't you guys just stick a movie on or something?' I suggest. 'Put *Frozen* on.'

Somehow, by the time Elsa unfreezes Arundel, my husband and I have managed to fit quilts, food, clothes, balls, scooters, skateboards, buckets, spades, surfboards, boogie boards and a tent into our car. We then stuff pillows and children into any available crevice and eventually hit the road. We look like the Clampetts from the *Beverly Hillbillies* as we reverse out of the drive.

I'm exhausted when we arrive at the site. I step out of the car and stare at a dusty clearing. Our home for the next three days. The kids fall out of the car, grab their scooters, and are off. My husband and I repeat the last four hours backwards, unpacking everything onto our desolate site.

We look each other in the eye as he pulls the tent from its bag. It's time. The construction of our fragile shelter. A task sadistic enough to end a marriage.

'Don't you fucking dare use your patronising "tent voice" with me,' I mutter through gritted teeth.

'I don't know what you're talking about,' my husband says as he saunters over to an area shadowed by a big gum tree.

Thus begins forty-five minutes of planning, erecting and hammering stakes. When it's all done, *I* realise *he* forgot to put down the damp-proof base.

'Don't worry about it, just leave it,' I say, ready for a cuppa.

'What if it rains?' he asks, pulling the stakes back out, one by one.

We're not talking by the time we inflate the blue mattresses two hours later.

*

The light is fading now, the sun swallowed by the tall eucalyptus trees surrounding our campsite. I watch as the sky shifts through shades of amber and pink. It's quiet for a moment, too quiet. Then it hits me. I'm alone. And all the children are missing. They've disappeared into newfound friends' tents or headed off to get stuck up a massive tree. I had told them to be back by six for dinner but it's nearly seven. I spend dusk wandering around the campground calling their names.

'Nelllll! Freeeddddd. Geeorge, where are you?'

There's a lump in my throat and the longer I can't find them, the more I presume they've been abducted. For me, camping equals worrying. There are so many death traps, endless hazards and people I don't like the look of. I can't relax when the children are lost in the dark with kids I don't know and places I haven't been.

After walking the entire length and breadth of the campground for an hour, trying to track them down, I return to our spot only to find them sitting in camp chairs eating hot dogs.

We wash up, then the kids shower and get ready for bed. I make a round of hot chocolates on the gas stove and we sit together in our camp chairs and play a game of charades in the moonlight. Seeing my children in their PJs, feet covered in sand, laughter spilling from their lips as they try to bring their favourite movies to life, fills me with a quiet warmth. In those fleeting moments the world falls away and it's just us and the stars. Time holds its breath, and I am lost in the simple magic of their joy, where nothing exists but the sound of their giggles and the glow of the night.

I pull a warm fluffy blanket over Fred, zip the other two into their soft sleeping bags, and whisper, 'It's time to go to sleep now.'

'We love camping, Mum,' mumbles Fred, just as he's drifting off.

'Yes, I love it too, camping's the best,' I lie.

I kiss each of their warm foreheads, unzip the flap, grab the car keys from the pocket of my husband's shorts, kiss him goodnight, jump into the car and speed (at eight kilometres per hour) away from that dusty campground.

This is how I cope. This is how I survive: I sneak off into the night and leave my husband there on his own. While they go back to nature, I go back to Netflix and a hot bath.

This is my top parenting hack: stay in a campsite within driving distance of home. (You're welcome.) It solves every issue. Everything is as it should be:

Them – freezing their arses off in a damp tent.

Me – home alone in a warm bed.

My kids have no idea I am gone. I return just as they wake, in time to cook bacon and eggs on that ridiculously tiny stove.

My hack ensures there is no angry, sleep-deprived tyrant in sight. Just a fresh-faced, rosy-cheeked supermum ready to shout 'car' every two seconds until bedtime.

I'm realising that this 'mumming' thing isn't always about being good at the things you hate doing – sometimes it's just about keeping up appearances, whether it's self-raising flour dusted across your nose, or sleeping in your own bed in order to stay present on a camping trip. There *are* loopholes that will make this long-haul parenting journey a little more manageable.

Just don't get caught.

Rabbit Droppings

It takes a few days to get back to normal after the camping trip. There is unending washing, the car has to be cleaned out and all the equipment stuffed back into cupboards. Just when I think I've settled back into the parenting groove, George decides he likes a girl at school.

'Mum, I'd like to invite Sara to go to the cinema with me this weekend.'

'Oh, right, okay.'

'Can you message her mum to ask her?'

'Erm yes, I can.'

Even though I say yes, my stomach swishes around. Anxiety unfolds itself, spreading from tip to toe as I have a rejection flashback, crying in a public loo after Mark Tilsly told me he'd 'rather go out with a rabbit dropping' than go out with me.

This prospective cinema date is the first inkling of interest in girls from my twelve-year-old and, even though I know it's time, I want to grab him and shout, *Don't do it! Save yourself! Run to the hills and become a eunuch or a cave-dwelling hermit. Not this! Anything but this.*

But, of course, I don't. I just spend an hour on Facebook stalking the girl's mother, deciding if her daughter is worthy of my boy's affection.

I never pause to consider if he is worthy of hers.

Sara's mum has all her teeth and there are no burnt couches, guns or fighting dogs in any of her profile pics, so I shoot her a message:

> Hello, Vic here, George's mum from school. George was wondering if Sara would like to go and see the Mario movie with him on Saturday. I will go with them and take them for a bubble tea afterwards. Happy to pick up and drop off.

Four little letters appear under the invite: *S E E N*. Then nothing. For hours. The wait is more painful than my husband ordering from a menu. (We all know you're having the fucking burger, for fuck's sake!) I check my phone every five seconds, unplug the router four times, refresh the page and pace. Surely it should be a quick answer, a simple decision.

I don't tell George about the delay in response. I flitter around, tidying up and humming insane lullabies to distract myself.

*

I remember the first date I went on, when I was only a little older than George. At thirteen, a boy called Peter from the year above me at the boys' school invited me to the cinema. I was scared, still very unsure of myself and how I looked. My hair was in that in-between stage, growing out the fringe and sideburns of an unflattering bowl cut, puppy fat still hung on to every bone and the braces on my teeth made me look like platform 7 at Paddington Station. My dad liked to refer to me by various names, which included 'Magnet Mouth' and 'The Human Cheese Grater'. Kids' braces in the 1980s were not like they are now, pretty colours or almost invisible. These were thick metal rods that ran across my teeth, with small elastic bands that attached the top braces to the bottom ones. Not very appealing at all. But I bravely decided it was time to escape the confines of my own face and get out there. All my friends had love interests, so I said 'yes' to Peter.

Mum dropped me off outside HMV, a record shop in Reading town centre, on a Saturday afternoon. When I approached Peter, wearing my baggy dungarees, a stripy black-and-yellow top that made me look like a bumblebee and so much make-up that I looked like I was on day release, he turned to say hello. His expression changed after a once-over: it went from cheery to looking as if a leaf-blower was being held directly in his face.

'What are you wearing that for?'

'It's my favourite outfit.'

'Please don't tell anyone about today.'

'Oh. Okay.'

He didn't talk much all afternoon. I bought both tickets to see *Edward Scissorhands* plus the popcorn, *and* he borrowed twenty-five pence for a Mars bar.

We went in and sat in the back row, knees touching. The glow of the big screen lit up his face and when I could, I turned to look at him. His eyes were very close together, he had hairs on his chin that my dad would have called 'bum fluff' and big flaring nostrils. His greasy hair was parted in the middle like an open encyclopedia and there were spots on his forehead. He wasn't good-looking at all, a bit ratty.

Halfway through the movie, he leant in and kissed me. It was quite nice at first. Just lips on lips. Then I felt his tongue trying to break through and force its way in. As I opened my mouth wide to accommodate his lashing tongue, the elastic bands that joined the top set of my braces to the lower ones snapped and pinged forward, from my mouth into his, causing him to choke momentarily. He sat back, gave me a funny look and then leant back in for more. For the next twenty-five minutes I allowed this boy to dispense saliva into my gaping mouth. At intervals some of the foamy dribble leaked out of the side and dripped into my ear hole. He grunted occasionally and my jaw ached. I wasn't sure what to do with my hands, so kept them firmly in my pockets. I felt sandpapery, spindly fingers reach inside my top and grab hold of my boob. He flicked at it like a broken light switch. I wanted to go home.

Afterwards, we sat on a wall outside the Odeon cinema, waiting for my mum to pick me up. Peter rolled the cog of a Zipper lighter up and down on his jeans. I noticed he had dirty fingernails and scabby hands. I heaved when he started to chew on a bit of dry skin on the side of his forefinger. I never wanted to see him again.

I didn't tell anyone that I had kissed this horrid boy. I just went and brushed my teeth for forty minutes, and then started a snog list in the back of my diary:

1. Peter H. Too slobbery. One tit. Bit of a 'rat boy'.

My list didn't get many more entrants that year. Unless cake was involved, my mouth stayed firmly closed. I decided to give boys a miss for a while, they didn't seem very nice and even though my mates at school seemed to like all this underwear fumbling and drooling on one another like randy Saint Bernards, I was more focused on playing Uno with my sister and swooning over posters of Morten Harket from a-ha. So, I waited and kissing boys took a back seat until the vision of manky Peter dissolved into my past.

Then I turned fourteen.

My hair was long, my shape was less fridge-like, the braces were off, and I was ready to undo my seatbelt and climb into the front seat. It was hard to meet boys. I went to an all-girls school. So, I had to be cunning at birthday parties and flutter my eyelashes as older brothers controlled the volume for musical statues. I had refined my flirtations practising in the bathroom mirror at home, as my windows of opportunity were so very small.

'Hi, I'm Vicky,' I said with dozy camel eyelids. 'Have you the new 5 Star album? It's well rad.'

My sister banged on the door.

'What are you doing in there, you weirdo?'

'Brushing my teeth. Bog off.'

The real ticket to ride was the invite to the annual disco at the parish hall, attached to the Catholic church. It was used for events like round table meetings, playgroup and women's circles. But once a year the smoke machine got dusted off, a dodgy DJ set up some decks and the local youth went wild.

Those kids' discos were like Roman orgies. Children falling out of bushes, faces stuck together; necking couples wrapped up in the velvet stage curtains, feet poking out the bottom. Spin the bottle was played in circles behind the pulpit, and doors of loos were wedged closed by mucky Adidas shoes as occupants grappled with buttons and zips. I had many firsts at these dirty discotheques: pash sessions in the graveyard, love bites in the cloisters (no, that's not another word for vagina) and dry humping in the vestry. The church doors were always open, and the creaky pews and rooms behind them were perfect for a snog marathon. I just had to make sure I didn't knock over a prayer candle or make eye contact with the baby Jesus while Ben Taylor was nibbling on my earlobe.

Before long there were other names under Peter. My snog list had grown.

2. Dave B. Nice eyes. Two tits. Bit of a bin sniffer.
3. Charlie. James T-shirt. Held hands. Marry.
4. Stephen R. Love bite.
5. Sasha D. Funny smell like Wotsits.
6. Micky. Sexy man in campsite. Two tits.
7. Matt. Train. Good kisser.
8. Creepy guy at Katie's party.
9. Simon. Tasted like Bovril.
10. Ben from disco. Tit nibble. Ear lick.

I did have some more-conventional dates as I got older. Some that were so forgettable that I forgot them, but there were many disasters that have stayed with me like a recurring nightmare. The most embarrassing being the time a pair of worn knickers (which were left in my jeans from the day before) fell out the bottom of my trouser leg when I was trying to impress a boy.

'What's that?' he asked, pointing at the flowery knickers now sitting on top of my trainer.

'Oh, I'm not sure.'

I kicked them into a bush and pretended it didn't happen, but he never called me again. I would have also liked to forget the time I disgraced myself in front of the school 'fitty', James Lewis. He was in the school art room on his own and I went over, holding a paintbrush, flicking my hair, looking all arty, and when I leant over the table to admire his drawing of a teapot, a little *parf* slipped out.

'Did you just fart?'

'No. Your chair moved.'

But my nose twitched, and any chances of a future betrothal dissipated into an eggy whiff. Still, I kept on, playing the field, hoping to fall in love. I got dumped by a hot electrician (there wasn't a spark anyway. Sorry!), two-timed by a set of twins (that was confusing), ditched by a DJ and spurned at a fairground in High Wycombe by a traveller boy for being a stuck-up private school twerp. I threw my hockey stick at him and told my friend Arabella I was 'never leaving Berkshire again'.

But nothing cut as deeply as Mark Tilsly and the rabbit dropping remark. I was so upset by his rebuff that I cried on my mum's lap for hours. I was fourteen and totally humiliated. So, it was then I decided to numb any future fumblings by guzzling cheap cider, beer and wine, and smoking so much weed that I thought the CIA were coming for me. Rejection was much easier to handle when I couldn't remember it. My romances were swift and usually involved nothing but an exchange of fluids and a fake phone number scribbled on a beer mat. I guess I was more of a 'get your coat, you've pulled' kind of dater. No real connection meant no real heartbreak.

I hope George's love life is a little less complicated than my own.

*

I hear a *ding*.

> Hey Vic, thanks so much for the invite. I've had a chat with Sara and she said she likes George as a school friend but does not want to go to the cinema with him. Thanks.

A spear has been plunged into my heart.

I find George watching TV. I sit down next to him and say, 'I just heard back from Sara's mum. She said Sara just wants to be friends and doesn't want to go to the cinema with you.'

Before he has time to react, I pull him into me, hoping to soak up his tears on my woolly jumper. 'Let it out, sweetie. Cry. I know it hurts, but this is life. Somebody will love you one day. I know it's hard but …'

I don't feel any sobs against my chest and there's no wailing or howling at the sky. All I hear is his muffled voice.

'Can you message Poppy's mum instead?'

Phew!

A week later, after a yes from Poppy, a question stops me in my tracks. I expect it, but I'm not ready for it.

'Mum, do storks really deliver babies down the chimney?'

Oh god. Here we go.

'No George, they don't. The postman shoves them through the letterbox or you can order them at McDonald's. Now, go and do your homework.'

'So, what's sex then?'

My toes curl up in my shoes.

Children knowing how they are made is a milestone I could do without. It would be much easier if they just carried on being kids, thinking babies grow on trees. But there is always that one kid at school who knows more than the rest and I have to intervene before they are given more wrong information.

Until I was eleven, I thought girls got pregnant by letting a boy put his tongue in their mouth, that an orgasm was something that lived in a rock pool, and a blow job was when you had your hair done at Carol's on High Street.

Then Emma Simpson in the year above told me about intercourse.

'No, it's not what you do after your GCSEs. It's sex, you know, when your dad puts his willy in yer mum.'

'Say that again?'

'Your dad puts his thingamajig in your mum's frontie.'

'What for?'

'That's how babies are made.'

Blood drained from my face.

What horrific news. Even my parents holding hands was enough to make me retch. How would I ever look them in the eyes again?

'WHAT'S THAT NOISE? ARE YOU ALL RIGHT VICTORIA?' Mum shouted up the stairs after school.

I didn't answer. I was too busy slamming my head in my wardrobe door trying to dislodge the image from my mind.

For some stupid reason I had thought kissing was the first and only port of call. I didn't know the downstairs department was involved or that there were other docks to moor the boat in, as it were. When my family and I sat together, dinners on trays on Sunday nights to watch David Attenborough programs, I presumed the monkeys were playing a game, climbing on each other's backs for a laugh. I remember my siblings smirking at each other as I said, 'Oh look, Mummy, the gibbons are having so much fun. Is that lipstick?'

And now here I am. Pointing the controller at the TV and turning it off if an ape gives so much as a suggestive glance. I don't want George to know – it means he's growing up.

Damn, I wish they had covered this at Sunny Days!

My own big sex talk at twelve was a bit of a cop-out. One night, I heard feet on the hallway outside my bedroom. The hallway light that seeped under the door darkened and I saw the corner of something white being pushed through the gap.

'Mum, I know you're there. What are you doing?'

I didn't get an answer and heard high heels clicking back down the stairs. I went over to the door and picked up a book. I sat on the end of my bed and opened it. Inside were drawings of wiggly sperm with smiley faces swimming towards an egg, a happy couple having a cuddle, a stubby little penis and a big hairy front bum. I had so many questions. But the mysterious delivery of the book suggested it wasn't something Mum wanted to discuss. My only informants were my sister and the older girls at school, and honestly, Emma Simpson was not a reliable source. She was always getting suspended for lying and spent a lot of assembly trying to lick her own eyebrows when she should have been reciting the Lord's Prayer.

We did do one sex education class at school. It was about an hour long. That was it. I remember putting my hand up and asking, 'Miss, does it hurt?' as I slid a condom over a banana.

'No, it should feel nice. That's why people keep doing it.'

I was horrified. It all seemed so yucky. So, I avoided sex until I knew exactly what it entailed. I was seventeen. I was drunk.

*

But George keeps on asking. My fake deafness, sudden fainting and bouts of unexpected diarrhoea will no longer distract him from his quest. He wants to know.

I go to the library and find the parenting section. There are so many choices of sex-ed books. Ones with pictures, ones with diagrams, ones that have a plastic covering and a CD attached to the inside cover. (I don't touch those ones.) I *am* pleased that all types of identities and families are represented on the shelves. It makes me proud to live in a world where people are free to love who they want to love.

Anyway, I choose one that has sperms with smiley faces, like the one I had as a kid but with a lot more 'sex facts' and content about making smart choices. I look over my shoulder as I slide it over the *beepy* checkout machine and then shove it in my bag like a copy of *Playboy.* I feel like a bit of a perv. But I am glad to have some answers for my kid burning a hole in my handbag.

It's time for me to step up and take sex education by the balls.

After the other kids go to bed, I get out the book I borrowed and call George into the lounge.

He sits between John and me and we turn to the first page.

'Oh god, Mum, am I about to have the sex talk?'

'Yes, you are. How much do you know?'

'I know mums and dads cuddle and that's how babies are made.'

'Well actually there's a bit more to it than that.'

'Can't I just look it up online?'

'NOOOOOOO! This is the one thing you should never look up online! NEVER, EVER DO THAT!'

As we turn the pages, George sits, shaking his head in disbelief. John and I take turns in reading and pointing at drawings. We get to the final page, which is a picture of a family around a bed with a rosy-cheeked mum holding a newborn. I am getting a bit emotional, wobbly at the wonder of procreation. I am hoping George has the same sentiment.

'Isn't it amazing, George?'

His head is in his hands.

'What you're telling me is … you and Dad did that … to make me. That is disgusting.'

'It's not disgusting. It's how people show their love for one another.'

But I've lost him. He looks up, face pale as a sheet, and says, 'Does that mean Granny and Grandad did that to make you?'

'No, they grew me on a tree. Now, off to bed.'

Ice Cream for Breakfast

As most parents of more than one child know, being 'one down' (as in one child going to a sleepover or having a playdate) is much easier than taking care of all of them … all at once. It lessens the chance for arguments, there aren't as many decisions to be made and there are fewer hungry mouths to feed. This small change in dynamics fills the house with calm. So, in order to be a special kind of mummy, I am trying to be more accepting about what happens when the kids sleep over at my parents' house.

'Did you brush your teeth at Granny's?' I ask when I pick George up and see all the sweet wrappers chucked on the floor.

'I never brush my teeth at Granny's.'

All the normal parenting guidelines go out of the cat flap when the grandparents take over. It's like dark forces descend and melt their brains. Against all my wishes, they shower the kids in sugar and I pick them up the next morning with bags under their eyes and the early stages of a urinary tract infection.

'Did you drink any water at Granny's, George?'

'No, just Coke.'

'But you know you're not allowed Coke!'

'Granny says I'm allowed.'

He spends the post-sleepover comedown trying to convince me that his dark mood is not because he went to bed at midnight after watching an M-rated monster movie with Grandad.

'I wasn't scared Mum, it was only a Marvel one – but can you keep the bathroom light on tonight?' he adds, before falling asleep at 7 pm.

My kids only ever used to see their grandparents on a screen. My parents lived in France and John's in the UK. Each week happy faces would Zoom in and read the kids a story, then tell us about the weather and various ailments they were all suffering from. But my mum and dad decided we were too far away so they moved, following us to Australia to live out their lives in the sunshine. We don't live far from them now. It's nice having them near. They get to have time with their grandchildren, and my husband and I are supplied with a never-ending amount of gossip fodder to discuss before bed.

'And Granny fell in the wheelie bin again.'

'Oh right, is she okay?'

'She's fine. Night night.'

'Night.'

Growing up, I lived quite far from my grandparents. William and Nellie Stubbs, my nan and grandad, lived on a council estate near Woking. Their house was on a corner, a red-brick building that looked like every other house on the street. The garden was edged with hawthorn bushes, and in spring the pathway to the front door was lined with daffodils. As soon as we passed the threshold, hot milk with a knob of butter was handed to my sister and me. The mug warmed my hands.

Their house, like a museum, preserved a gramophone on a mahogany sideboard, ornaments of shepherds on dusty shelves above the electric fireplace, potpourri that smelt of nothing in the centre of the dining table. My grandad, in his rocking chair, an unmoving relic himself, would be sipping on an inch of whisky, silently staring at the box.

My sister Sarah and I put on shows, dancing around the living room draped in embroidered tablecloths we found in the bottom drawer of Nan's hallway cabinet, each of us pretending to be a bride or a ghost. We played hide-and-seek and ran to the kitchen for what seemed a never-ending supply of gingernut biscuits.

We didn't sleep over very often because the freezing bedroom with peeling floral wallpaper scared us. The top layer revealed old 1930s drawings of the Mother Goose poem

'Hey Diddle, Diddle' with an evil spoon-man running off with a plate that had curly hair. This stuff of nightmares had me quivering in fear and pulling an itchy blanket over my head. Metal-framed windows banged in the wind, cold air seeped under the door and the floor creaked with every step. My sister and I slept with our socks on, top to tail with a hot water bottle nestled between to keep us warm. Nan brought hot chocolates and placed them on a doily on the bedside table and read *Aesop's Fables* and *Little Red Riding Hood* from old books with yellowed pages and flaking spines.

Our most loved stories were the ones Nan told us about growing up in East London during the war. Nan said they sang songs to keep up morale and drown out the sound of the bombs going off. She worked delivering food during World War II and rode her bike along the Thames. I imagined her as a young woman, bumping along the cobbled streets waving at people she knew with one hand and holding her hat on her head with the other, as she freewheeled down the street.

At every family party, Nan sang 'Crazy' by Patsy Cline in a trembling voice that made me cry. I could tell it reminded her of being young. She was way into her eighties by then, but Nan could still rock 'n' roll. When Chubby Checker came on the jukebox, one of her grown-up sons would say, 'Come on, Mum.' And her tiny frame would shuffle onto the dancefloor. Her mouth changed when she was spun around, from pursed lips to wide open. I used to mimic her facial expressions from my spot on the sofa and watch her bingo wings (the loose skin under her arms) flap as she moved. One song was enough for her spindly legs, and she spent the rest of the party with her feet up on a piano stool, sipping a glass of sherry.

'Nice moves, Nan.'

'I've still got it.'

I have fond memories of Christmas Eves at that house. We'd sit at her Formica table in the kitchen making decorations out of pinecones, cottonwool and silver elastic. Grandad's noises echoed throughout the house as he pulled the ladder down from the loft, then shouted with his head inside the black hole, 'Which lights do you want out, Nellie? Do you want the whole nativity set? It looks like a mouse got into it and shat on the three kings.'

Torn cardboard boxes were handed down and dumped near the tree. My sister and I hung so many glass fairies, acorn Santa heads, baubles and tinsel on the branches that they slid off, one by one, scattered around the base, where the cat peed on them.

Mum told me that when I was a baby, Nan dipped my dummy in a glass of Scotch whisky on Christmas Day. It was my special treat.

'She'll sleep like a log, Maureen,' she said to my aghast mother. I wasn't freaked out by the creepy wallpaper on those nights. Out like a light.

My nan died a couple of months before my wedding. I would like to say I sat at her bedside, held her hand and told her how much I loved her as she closed her eyes and took her last breath. The truth is, I was drunk the last time we spoke and have a vague memory of slurring the first verse of 'The White Cliffs of Dover' down the phone for no apparent reason. But it hasn't clouded the memories I've kept of her. Pound coins taped inside birthday cards. Her fuzzy hair. Hot milk, tight cuddles and warm feet.

'Night, night. Sleep tight and don't let the bed bugs bite,' she would say as she pecked each of us on the nose.

'Good night, Nanny.'

We didn't sleep over at William and Dora's, my dad's parents' place, very often either. Gran said she was too old to be responsible for us (she was sixty). We just went for afternoon tea, served in blue-and-white china cups, and left with the pockets of our skirts dragging along the ground filled with copper coins emptied out from Grandad's NatWest piggy bank. They sometimes came to stay with us though, Grandad sat in a chair reading a big broadsheet paper while Gran reminisced about 'walking the boards' at the Guildford Amateur Theatre Association. She had always wanted to be an actress and they put on a different play every week. I remember seeing her dressed as Queen Victoria once, stomping around the stage, in a big black dress and bonnet. She was always the star of the show.

Towards the end of her life, we took her to a carol-singing service, in a field. We wheeled her over the mud in a wheelchair because the ground was wet and uneven. Halfway through, just as we finished singing 'Oh Come, All Ye Faithful', she stood up, threw her hands in the air and shouted, 'It's a miracle! I can walk!' The whole crowd cheered and we got free toffee apples.

My gran was so witty and quick. I looked up to her, admired her eccentricities. I still live by one of her sayings, 'A dirty mind is a joy forever.' Which I now know she stole off Oscar Wilde, but I'm sure it sounded better coming from Gran.

Whenever I saw either sets of grandparents as a kid, there were no rules either. I was spoilt. Sneakily handed five-pound notes when my mum wasn't looking. Given paper bags full of sweets, gummy teeth and fizzy colas. Taken to the park on warm summer nights when I should have been in bed. My grandparents loved treating us. Our relationship was built on affectionate cheek pinches, cuddles, spare change, funny songs and sweets.

*

My kids' visits to their own grandparents are now staggered. They won't have all three. That's the rule. One at a time. (I wish I could have one at a time too.)

At Granny's house, all other rules are as murky as dishwater. They are allowed to eat whatever they want. Marshmallows for lunch, candy canes for afternoon tea and a packet of dried noodles for dinner.

When I first began letting the kids sleep over, I was confused. Surely if I say bed by 8 pm and no ice cream, the elders of the family must adhere to what the womb provider asks? But as time passed and my family grew, I understood a night off, even if it's only one child gone, is worth the sucrose fallout. My parents let my kids do whatever they want when they are with them. It's just how they keep them quiet and onside. I suppose they don't run off or break things when a tray of donuts, six cans of Fanta and *Monty Python and the Holy Grail* are on offer.

When I think about it, I do the same thing. If other people's kids are at my house, I let them watch movies and eat crap. I give them lollies and fizzy drinks, plates of Doritos and icy poles. I spoil them. I watch them run around like maniacs while I nibble on a bowl of nuts.

There is a sort of, 'Well, they're not my kids, I don't give a fuck what they eat' attitude. All my good parenting disintegrates because I want them to have fun and go back to their mates saying:

'Nell's mum made us cupcakes for lunch! I had the best day ever.'

And this is why my kids have a better time at my parents' house than they do at their own.

They prefer going to a place where they can do and eat what they want and watch the iPad until their eyeballs drop out from their sockets. It's much more fun than being in the house with the grumpy lady who has a TV time limit and makes them eat carrot coins.

But it's not all ice cream for breakfast at my parents' house. Grandad plants herbs in the garden with Fred, plays with dolls with Nell and takes George to the bike track. Granny potters around in the kitchen and appears every half-hour with plates of flaky homemade sausage rolls. Her favourite outing is a trip to the op shop with the kids, where she let's them buy whatever they want. They come home with net bags filled with Barbie limbs, board games with no dice, smelly princess dresses with stains on them and malevolent-looking china dolls. Granny's house is like a utopia where everything I've tried to teach my kids – morals, rules, ethics – slides down the drain for that one special night … and I'm left to suck it all back up with a metaphoric plunger the following day.

My husband's mum isn't quite as flimsy with rules. Flat-Nanny from the iPad comes to life once a year. She arrives at our local airport, after a long-haul flight, and is met by three rhinos charging towards her.

'Nann-eeeeee!'

She drops to her knees and all three kids manage to fit into her embrace. I see tears streaming down her face. Either Fred winded her or she's crying with joy. Flat-Nanny brings in her luggage one jumper, walking shoes and a life jacket, 'Just in case.' The rest of the space is stuffed with craft supplies. The kids spend three weeks making puppets, paper masks and painting by numbers. My husband and I use up a year's worth of babysitting, and by the time Nanny leaves Nell can sew, George knows algebra, Fred can bake fairy cakes and I've put on five kilos. I decide she can come again. The more parenting she does, the less I have to.

My kids adore all their grandparents. Their presence makes them feel safe. It reminds me of how I felt when I was at my nan's. Cosy, in a home filled to the brim with sweets and emptied out of rules. A house where there's always enough time for a story … and where love is hidden in chocolate buttons.

'The Man'

I'm at the local café today, trying to grab a coffee without having an argument. Fred isn't at school today, he said he felt tired, so I've let him have a day off. 'A mummy day' as we like to call it. Last night, I didn't seem like the baddie for once: I had let him stay up late, eat brownies and watch *Wipeout!* with me. I acted all chummy mummy rather than authoritarian. Trying to be the 'Sunny Days Parent' *all the time* is draining and slightly depressing.

I'm up at the counter handing over my card. I thought Fred was playing with some toys in the corner but when I turn, I see him standing in the centre of the café, naked.

'Erm, sorry about this,' I say to the café worker as I pick Fred's underpants up off the floor. Then to Fred, 'That's a three … two … one …'

He ignores me. He's laughing and starts running around. Customers stare. Instead of leaving him there or pretending I don't know who he is, I try again.

'Three, two … and that's a one. If you don't come here and put your underwear back on, you will lose TV time for a week.'

I'm looking him in the eyes. He does a big toothless grin and a little bum wiggle. I have to hold in my laugh.

Time to bring in the big guns. Reinforce some order before a 'mutiny on the mothership'.

I tell him very seriously, '"The Man" is coming.'

As I say it, I picture the lady with the nice earrings shaking her head in disappointment. I know it's bad mumming, but I have run out of numbers.

Fred's eyes dart about, his face goes pale and beads of sweat appear on his tiny forehead as he tries to spot a shadowy figure lurking somewhere nearby.

Even though my children have never seen 'The Man', the mere thought of his existence is enough to have them shaking in their Crocs. His potential proximity corrects disruptive behaviour and levels out even the most violent meltdowns. Within seconds, pants are back on and Fred is hugging my shins.

They never ask who 'The Man' is or why he is skulking near every café, park, playground, house or restaurant in our neighbourhood. They just accept that if he does appear, the consequences will be horrifying.

'The Man' stems from my own youth. A man lived near my primary school who we called 'Mad Man Fowler'. He wore a flat cap and thick-rimmed Buddy Holly–style glasses. We shouted, 'Mad Man Fowler's coming!' from the sports field as he shuffled towards the bus stop with a Waitrose plastic bag banging against his calf. It looked as if he was carrying a small decapitated head. He mumbled to himself, like he had an angry pixie sitting on his shoulder, tormenting him. His head was always at an awkward angle, as he spat inaudible profanities from the corner of his mouth.

Each day, Fowler caught the Number 27 bus to Oxford at 10.15 am. For unknown reasons, I decided he was heading to work in a coalmine, even though the nearest coalmine was 500 miles away, in Wales, and closed in 1927. When we spotted him at playtime, the whole of 2B (Mrs Buxton's class) shouted, 'Look! Mad Man Fowler is off down the pits. RUN!' And as we legged it in the opposite direction, we all laughed so hard that we collapsed in the wet grass near the bike sheds.

Fear and giggles whipped up together was exhilarating at that age. If it wasn't Mad Man Fowler, it was an axe-wielding crazy person from a horror story banging a severed arm of a murdered nurse on the bonnet of her car. This was the stuff of thrills that kept us awake at night.

I realise now that Mad Man Fowler was just a bloke in a hat off to visit a mate, going to work, or taking a jacket potato to his sick mother. He wasn't mad at all. He was grumbly because twenty-six children gawked at him every morning, faces filled with giddy horror, running away screaming and laughing. It couldn't have felt very nice. *Sorry, Mr Fowler.*

*

There are three reasons I scare my children with 'The Man'. Firstly, when I have no control over them. Secondly, when I am lazy. And thirdly, when they don't listen to me.

When your five-year-old has his penis on display in public, the quickest option is to yell, '"The Man" is coming!' The electric shock of his approach zaps Fred into paying attention. It's the shortcut I need to allow us to leave the café quickly.

I don't feel bad about using this frightening figure to aid my parenting because a friend of mine uses 'The Gulligan', a monster who lives under the bed of children who don't sleep. Another has the 'Rain Troll'. He bangs on windows if you get up in the night. And a lady in Mothers' Group has a 'Bedroom Hobgoblin' who telephones the headmaster when clothes are not put away. It turns out the cast of *Lord of the Rings* are hiding in cupboards, laundry baskets and under beds of naughty children everywhere. The only thing that I do feel bad about is that it could be making my children scared of all men. I thought about making my threat a bit more inclusive but '"The Person" is coming' just doesn't have the same ring to it.

Having a few monsters in my back pocket is a useful tool. I'm at the 'Whatever it takes' stage of parenting where deceiving my children, daily, is how I survive. Lying has become so commonplace that I don't even realise I'm doing it.

'The beach is closed,' I say without flinching. 'A killer jellyfish washed up this morning. It was on the news. All the beaches on the Sunshine Coast are shut.'

'Can we go to the cinema then?'

'There's nothing on – just a bird-watching documentary.'

It's *The Angry Birds Movie*. But sitting through another kids' flick about an animal that gets rejected by its herd/pride/circus/family is not an option. Nor do I have any sympathy for the lost dogs of Disney. Then there's the game of musical chairs on arrival, the inevitable popcorn explosions, unmanageable toddlers roaming the aisles, the sound straws make when pulled out of giant cups of Sprite. It's enough for me to ban all cinema visits from here to eternity.

'What about the indoor play centre, Mummy?'

'It shut down because someone got their head stuck in the cargo net. And anyway, you may as well go and wash your face in the toilet.' That place is a petri dish of multiplying bacteria. A snot graveyard. The only upside of an indoor play centre is that you leave with an immunity to measles.

One of my other favourite lies happens when they emerge each day from the classroom clutching a fist full of paper.

'Look what I did, Mummy. It's a unicorn,' Nell says.

I take the wrinkled A4 sheet bearing a brown splodge with one eye and a kind of weird mono leg.

'That's wonderful – what a brilliant drawing. What's this one?'

I unfurl the paper.

'This one is my favourite, Mummy. It's a pig dragging a girl.'

'Right. Okay. That's very clever.'

I can make out the pig and some red crayon, which I presume is the girl's blood.

I pat my daughter on her head and say, 'Well done.' But I'm wondering if I need to mention it to the 'special doctor', along with her invisible mates.

Then there's the white lies:

'The ice cream van's song means they've run out.'

'All the little chickens stopped laying mini chocolate eggs since Covid.'

'Staring at your iPad for too long will make your eyes square.'

'If you don't eat vegetables, you turn into a toad.'

Sometimes I lie just because I enjoy it.

We recently went on a trip to Great Keppel Island in Queensland and I told the children for weeks in advance that it was home to the famous 'Great Keppels' – a sweet speciality dish only found in this unique destination.

'They grow on trees and taste like donuts.'

'We can't wait to try the keppels, Mum. It's going to be the yummiest thing ever.'

I snuck into the hotel's kitchen before breakfast on the first day and asked the staff to create a keppel for me. They covered a carrot in chocolate sauce and giggled as they carried the plates from the kitchen. The children had napkins tucked into the top of their T-shirts and sat holding knives and forks on their ends, waiting for the local speciality to arrive.

'Here you go kids! Your keppels!'

I like to recall their disappointed faces whenever I need cheering up.

I also lie about myself. I tell them I was a grade-A student and I never bunked off school, never stole money from my dad's wallet, never woke up in the bucket of a digger after a night out in Magaluf, or god forbid, had a sip of booze. I'm keeping them in the dark about my misdemeanours, hoping they don't turn out like me.

'Mummy, did you ever smoke?'

'No darling. Smoking is dangerous.'

Lying, as if I didn't know, was a very bad idea. It seemed like the easy way out in the early days, a quick fix to get them in the car, or a trick to help me regain control. My lies seemed innocent and fun. But I now realise it's bloody stupid, a flying arrow of consequence, turning around mid-air and heading straight back at me.

I have raised a family of fabricators. There are so many lies being flung around that I don't know which way is up. Trust has become wobbly.

Fred lies about food. He looks up at me with those big brown eyes and denies scoffing all my Lindt balls, even though there are wrappings scattered around his feet and chocolate smeared all over his face. George lies about how long he's been on the Nintendo Switch. The dog even lies, sauntering past little puddles of piss as if she knows nothing about them.

*

I manage to get Fred dressed and we have a lovely day together. I take him to do the weekly shop, we head to the beach where we jump waves and he even has an afternoon nap. I have to stroke his cheek to wake him for school pick-up.

Once dinner is done and the house is relatively calm, my phone *dings*.

—Hi Vic, how's Nell? It must have been so scary for you all.
Sending lots of love.
—Sorry I don't know what you're talking about.
—We heard about Nellie and the snake bite. The whole school is talking about it.
—What snake bite?

I call a few mums and make further enquiries. It turns out that on arrival at school that morning, Nell had told everyone that she had stepped on a snake in the garden on Saturday afternoon and it had bitten her. She was so convincing that even the teachers believed her. I know because they are messaging me too.

Ding.

So glad Nell is okay. What a nightmare. So brave. From class 2K.

Ding.

Nell, you hero! You must all be so relieved.

I call her down to the lounge.

'Nell, can you come here for a minute please?'

She looks so innocent, her hair up in cute bunches, as she slides towards me, using her socks like skis to cross the wooden floor.

'Please tell me it's a mistake and you didn't tell your entire class you were bitten by a red-bellied black snake and spent the whole weekend in hospital?' I ask with a serious tone.

'No.'

'Are you lying to me, Nell?'

'No, Mum.'

Her face is serene. Angelic.

112

I notice a big band-aid stuck to her left calf.

'Are you sure? Nellieeeeee?'

Her lip starts to wobble.

'You need to tell me the truth, Nell. It's okay, I won't be angry.'

'I'm sorry, Mummmyyyyyy ...'

She goes on to tell me it was all meant to be a joke, it just got out of hand. I can't help but feel sorry for her. I'm also secretly impressed. It's a good story, believable, but I know a pat on the back for being so imaginative is not the answer here.

When she's finished explaining the whole situation, she squeezes her eyes closed, preparing herself for a thunderous telling-off. But I don't shout. I just give her a big cuddle, and as she sobs in my arms I can't help thinking this is completely my fault. Telling all those little white lies has rubbed off.

Oh gosh. Will I ever be able to undo all the harm I've done? Maybe it's too late for me to be a better parent?

As Nell's crying slows down, I decide to set free the remaining monsters hiding in my back pocket. No more lies.

She looks up at me, her pretty blue eyes shining with tears, and I explain that she will have to go to school in the morning and admit it was all made up. I explain why lying can be dangerous and how it can break trust. I'm saying it to myself too, trying to absorb my own advice.

'I know it might seem easier, or more interesting to lie but it will get you in more trouble in the long run, Nell.'

'Okay, sorry, Mum.'

'It's okay. Now, can you go and finish off your bedroom?' Her room has been a mess for weeks, and cleaning it might give her the space she needs to think about her behaviour – and I feel like I have parented well by giving her a consequence.

'Okay.' She says and wanders off down the hallway.

About twenty minutes later, after not hearing a peep out of her, I go to her bedroom and find her curled up on her bed with a little blanket over her, fast asleep. Her room is still a complete tip. I consider waking her and getting her to finish it …

But I don't.

I take a deep breath.

Be the mummy you know you can be, Vic.

I decide to save myself an argument. I kneel and start picking up beads from the floor. I fold the clothes that were strewn around the room and put them away in her wardrobe. I line her teddies up against the wall and quietly clean up her little dresser, so all her nail varnish and make-up is organised, ready to use. Then I perch on her bed, stroke her forehead, and hum a little lullaby.

For once, 'The Man' didn't come.

Mummy did.

A Wapple

May

Even though it's autumn Down Under, there's a spring in my step. The kids haven't thrown any glue sticks at my head this week and my parenting seems to have blossomed.

Nell was brave and told everyone at school about the snake lie and even made a few new friends. She never ceases to amaze me. One minute she's crying into my jumper, the next she's making daisy chains. I wish I could be more like her.

Nell is the world's best, best friend. If she's not making an 'I Love You' bracelet out of rainbow beads, she's buying adjustable emoji rings and BFF fluffy hairbands at the market. Nell thinks about her friends all the time.

'Can Eve come over please, Mum?'

'I need to have a sleepover with Mimmie. It's my turn.'

'Sadie wants to make tie-dye T-shirts with me. Please, Mummy?'

It never ends.

One of Nell's many best friends, Mim, was born on the same day as her. They're like two happy puppies when they're together. Bouncing around, playing, bumbling along next to each other yapping about nails and hairstyles. Nell is deeply loyal and kind to Mim. The sort of friend who would pick you up from the airport at 3 am with a smile and not even ask for petrol money. But apart from her little girl gang, Nell, it turns out, has other types of friendships too …

Today, I experience a 'wapple'. According to Nell, a wapple is when you play with someone you've never met before and then never see them again.

We are at the wake park when it happens, watching George swoosh round the lake on his board. I see Nell sidle up to a boy who is buying some hot chips at the counter.

'Hello. I'm Nell,' she says, offering him her hand.

They spend the next twenty minutes playing tag.

Sometimes I wonder if I am here to teach my children or if they are here to teach me. Not only has Nell made up a word, she's also confident enough to fulfil its sentiment. Her ability to make new friends is inspiring. She does it with such ease. What really moves me is how she is unquestionably herself. No airs or graces. She doesn't change herself to appease the chosen 'wapple'. She just says 'hi' and it flowers from there.

A new friend is made and never to be seen again.

'I love wapples, Mum,' she says.

George is on his last lap of the lake, so I coax Nell away from her new buddy with the promise of an icy pole.

'Come on Nellie, say goodbye to your new friend.'

As she walks over, the boy's mother and I do an 'aren't they sweet' fake smile at each other, and I very briefly consider a wapple myself, but I don't want to impose or seem desperate, so I just do a weird wave … then leave.

George, still in his wetsuit, comes over and we all sit in a line, sucking our icy poles until the ice goes white. We turn the little plastic sleeves upside down to slurp the syrupy juice at the same time.

'Can we wapple again tomorrow, Mum?'

'Of course we can.'

As I pack wet towels into the big beach bag, I let out a big sigh.

'Are you all right, Mummy?'

'We are so alike in some ways, Nellie, and so different in others.'

I find friendships a struggle. Some old mates miss the party girl who had good stories and new mates probably find me a little dull. A few casualties have dropped off the friendship radar in the past few years. The huge change in me, from drunk mummy to sober mummy, was too much to bear. People just don't want an abstemious fizzy-water weirdo hanging off their coat tails on a night out, and drinking orange squash at pissy playdates is why I don't get invited back. The way I socialise now could be mistaken for a wake. All I can offer is a biscuit, a cup of tea and a nice chat.

I'm getting used to the occasional rejection. It doesn't set off the people-pleaser within anymore or send me down a 'why does everybody hate me?' mental spiral, it just sets me up for a night in and a luxury cheese board all to myself.

I'm at that stage in life where I don't think I need any more mates. I still have my solids. The pillars of strength and constancy. The friends who are there, standing strong like Roman columns in my life. The cobbers, the supporters, the texters and the callers. The mummy mates who never falter. I can count my close friends on one hand, but in that palm sit shiny diamonds. Having these firm friendships means I no longer put effort into new ones. Making friends is all a bit hard and awkward.

It doesn't help that I don't really go anywhere. I don't go in at school drop-off as much anymore and I avoid playgroup like the plague. Playgroup makes me feel old. I had Fred at forty-two. In hospital I had to wear a red shower cap and had the words 'geriatric mother' scribbled on a board above my bed. I was surprised the nurse didn't ask me about the war. On my last visit to playgroup, I left feeling depressed after watching young mums kneel next to toddlers on floor mats – they didn't even groan when they got up! Some of the grandmas chatted to me as if I was in their crew. 'It's nice when you can give them back, eh?' 'Are you in GemLife?'

Spending ten years at the same playgroup puts an end to any enthusiasm over a high tower of plastic blocks, painting of a massive blob and a wooden puzzle that smells of vomit. Reading *That's Not My Monkey* while a toddler chokes on apple slices just doesn't cut it for me anymore. I can't do 'How old is Lily now?' and 'Do you live locally?' exchanges. I'd rather hide in a corner on a low table and construct a life-size Trojan horse out of lollipop sticks.

Playgroup is done, so nowadays I stay at home and write. Being home is okay, but recently I've started talking to myself and gnawing at my own elbow. I sit each day at my computer wondering what to eat next to distract me from my own existence. Days drag and my writing has nothing inspiring to draw from. The only book I could possibly write would be based upon bin day, magpie squawking patterns and the hot delivery guy.

After Nell's interaction at the wake park and as part of the 'better mumming' endeavour, I decide to get back out there and make some new friends. Wapple. I'm going to step into who I really am for once and find some mates with a common interest.

I see the advert flapping in the wind, pinned to a board outside Coles, and pull off the paper phone number. It's for a writing group at the local community centre every other

Monday. The advert says: *Bring a name badge, a pen and paper and under a thousand words to read out. Poems or prose.* I find an old blog post I've written and print if off.

*

I arrive at the glass door and stop to take a deep breath before I go in. But before I can push it open an older man with kind eyes pulls the door inwards and says, 'Hello, I'm Denzil. You must be Victoria. Come in and take a seat.'

I glance around and say hello to the other people. I'm the youngest, but I'm not fazed; I'm looking forward to knowing about these people and hearing how they interpret the world. My eyes focus on the wooden lectern in the corner of the room and my palms become sweaty as I take my seat.

'Welcome to the Sunshine Coast Writers' Group. Now who wants to go first?'

A guy with a Scandinavian accent shoots up his hand. 'I will.'

He makes his way over to the lectern holding a folded sheet of paper. He spreads the paper open and begins to read.

What unfolds before me for the following two hours is simply perfect.

I sit back as the words of others flow over me. One lady reads a poem about a trip away and I close my eyes as I absorb her descriptions of the English countryside, hollyhock-lined country paths and ivy-covered cottages. A man in his eighties reads a poem about unrequited love and I feel my heart ache alongside his. A guy in motorbike boots describes the Australian outback with such clarity I can almost feel the red earth between my toes. There are tales from World War II, dystopian futures and broken pasts. One lady reads a haiku that is so eloquent I want to cry. And just when I think I can't feel any more, a guy I hadn't noticed gets up and reads a chapter of a book he is writing about his life. He doesn't look up. He can't. It's too personal. He is dressed all in black with a looming presence that takes up the room, his story filling any remaining space. It's so powerful I can hardly breathe. Prison. Fear. Judgement. Mental health. The weight of his words heavy upon us all.

We break for a cup of tea.

I pour boiling water over a tea bag and have a sense of missing out. I can't believe this has been going on under my nose, at my local community centre, and I didn't know about it. I've been stuck at home, feeling old, lonely and a bit unmotivated, when stories were floating from a window nearby.

We head back in and it's my turn. My hands shake when I reach the lectern. I read the blog post. I rush through, wanting it to be over. It gets a little clap and I return to my chair.

'Does anyone have any feedback on Victoria's story?' Denzil asks.

'I really enjoyed it.'

'Yes, very descriptive. I like the bit about your family.'

'Well done, Vic. You see, it wasn't that bad!' says Denzil.

A few more people read before I leave for school pick-up. I whisper a quiet 'thank you', not wanting to interrupt the final speaker and sneak out the door. What an afternoon. I'm humbled to be among such inspiring people.

As I sit in the carpark at school waiting for the kids, I look at my phone. A notification sits there. It's for a gig, a boozy night out which I know I will hate. My mind flashes forward, me not being able to hear people, inane nodding, annoying split bills, checking my watch under the table, planning my escape and then having to wait for dribbly mates to drive home. I do it all because I want to prove I'm not boring.

Look everybody! I'm still fun!

I stare ahead, breathe in, and click *Not Going.*

You'd think a people-pleaser declining an invite would trigger a flash mob. I scan the carpark, a couple of mums chatting, some toddlers running in and out of a ditch. No fluorescent spandex, leg warmers or high kicking to 'Nothing's Gonna Stop Us Now' by Starship in sight. I'm disappointed, but a funny feeling stirs in my tummy.

Maturing is excruciating when you've never experienced it before.

I have boundaries now. Who knew?

Clicking *Not Going* represents me taking care of myself, putting *me* first. I'm no longer appeasing others to fit in, throwing out daggy dance moves to prove a point. It's a milestone.

When my husband gets home, he asks, 'Why are you looking so pleased with yourself?'

'I had a lovely afternoon and I said *no* to going to a party. I've realised I can make new friends without feeling like a total loser! I just need to meet people who like the same things I do.'

My eyes fill with tears.

'What's the date today? Is your period due?'

After punching my husband in the bollocks, I grab my laptop and create a meet-up group for sober women. I organise a 'bring a plate' picnic the following weekend. Eight women come.

We talk about alcohol, about our families and about our crazy lives before. Sober people have a reputation for being boring, but we are the ones with the good stories. One of the ladies told us how she once jumped on a horse and rode it bareback around a field when off her nut. Another woman about the time she shot someone with an air rifle and lied to the police. Someone else dived into a lobster tank at a work function. I tell them about blowing my finger off with a firework on the millennium night and how once I was driven out of a resort in Thailand by the managers and told to never return after I kicked a door in during a blackout. Out of nowhere a woman who had not spoken yet says:

'Bloody hell. I thought I was bad, but you lot were all fucking lunatics!' and we all fall about laughing.

It isn't all giggles though. With struggles come tears. We share our turning points, the moments we decided to change, and we listen as some ask questions: 'Why can't I stop doing something I hate?' and 'What's wrong with me?' The women are all vulnerable, and sharing our experiences really makes me feel heard. The following week, I organise a walk to the lighthouse in Mooloolaba, then a dinner at the local Indian restaurant, and soon I have an entire group of friends who don't drink. The best thing about it is there's no pressure to be anyone but myself.

My little outings, writing groups, boot camps, sober groups and a few dinners out with the solids prove to me that I don't need friendship in the traditional sense. I just need a few rewarding connections.

And perhaps the odd wapple.

Explain Cut and Paste

I'm at an outdoor water play area near my mum and dad's. There are fountains, tubes with spouts of water shooting out and a big bucket that tips over every few minutes. Instead of wapples, I am hanging out with people I know. The young ones and the old ones.

My mum is sitting in the pergola, checking her watch, and I'm watching the kids. They're running around. Wet hair stuck to faces, little water droplets on the end of their eyelashes, leaping over columns of water, and stepping on the holes in the ground, stopping its flow. Bodies shiver when the wind blows through. My three rugrats run up to me at intervals, grab towels off me like I'm the old hat stand in the corner of my nan's front room, then after a cuddle and a warm-up, head back in for another drenching.

'Victoria. Can we go yet? I'm having the ladies-over-sixty group for dinner tonight and I haven't got the fish pie out of the freezer yet. Oh, and when you drop me off, can you check the garage? There's a funny smell, like a corpse is rotting in the fancy dress box. Don't worry, it's not your father.'

Then a voice from the other direction.

'Muuum, Fred is doing a wee in the drain.'

I see my youngest standing in the middle of the water play area, people all around him, holding his willy. He's looking up, smiling at me.

Oh god, not again.

'Okay, we will go in a sec, Mum, let me just sort these kids out first.' I dump damp clothes next to her and rush towards the children.

'Fred, that's not okay. We're going.'

'I don't want to go.'

'Get the others. We're off.'

'I hate you.'

'And I love you. Now let's go.'

'Come on Victoria, I think I've got a parcel arriving soon and I don't want to miss the postman. He's from Poland you know.'

'I'M COMING MUM!' I say to her and then turn and shout towards the water play area again.

'PLEASE GUYS, LET'S GET A MOVE ON!'

I'm yelling, but the inhabitants are all at a silent disco, dancing to their own tune.

No one comes. I trudge over, pull Fred's arm. George traipses up behind and as Nell's hand slips into mine, she mutters, 'I don't want to go. You're the worst mummy ever.'

My mum sidles up.

'I would have never talked to my mother like that.'

I sigh, say nothing and shepherd the flock in the direction of the car. I strap in little bodies, hand out snacks, and drive with my mum in my ear telling me about her friend who's put on weight. 'It's such a shame. She's really let herself go.' I want to say to her that it's not okay to talk about people's body size, but I can't be bothered arguing and the great unsaid makes me anxious inside.

Some days everyone needs me. I am an island between two generations. My parents have reached old age and my children just starting out. It's a place where responsibility weighs heavy, where lives flow like brackish water, mixing when they need to, parting when their time comes.

When I am with the kids *and* my parents it's like I'm in a tug of war. Everyone is pulling me towards them, in need of attention, and I'm expected to know the answers. My patience is stretched like cling film, the flimsy veil not covering anyone enough to make them feel completely protected. Having three kids and elderly parents is forever being at the end of the roll.

At Mum's, I discover that her freezer has stopped working.

'Dad must have done it. He was fiddling with the buttons.'

She pokes her finger into a tub of ice cream and then the now-runny fish pie.

'Well, the over-sixties lot can't eat that. Dad can have that for his dinner. I'll just have a couple of my biscuits.'

I get a bin bag and dump the fish pie and all the food that's defrosted. I mop up water that has leaked out the bottom and as I push down on the mop to squeeze the excess water out into the bucket, I close my eyes.

I had told them to buy a new freezer, and not get one second-hand off Facebook Marketplace just because 'it looked brand new'. But things like this and hasty purchases are a common theme when you're over eighty.

'We're getting a convertible,' Mum blurts out one morning. 'A red one with a go-faster stripe down the side.'

John looks over from the printer in the corner of my parents' lounge. It's making noises like a pterodactyl that's been snatched out of the sky by a T-rex. There is a wad of paper an inch thick stuck in the inner workings of the machine.

'C'mon you little fucking fuck stick.'

It's not just dealing with dodgy freezers when we go to my parents' house. It's a weekly roundup of tech support. It goes like this:

1. Teach them how to use the smart TV.
2. Explain why restoring phones to factory settings once a week is bad.

3.   Clarify why they can't download *MasterChef* from
     the BBC iPlayer.

4.   Go over how to 'send a letter' on Facebook.

5.   Search for Dad's Kindle, which he thinks he left at the
     café in Bunnings. (It's always down the side of the couch.)

6.   Explain cut and paste.

7.   Spend three hours trying to unravel why they have
     changed all their passwords: 'There's something
     wrong with my Hotmail, John. It's locked me out.
     I didn't do anything.'

I make tea and watch my husband move between devices. It doesn't matter what it is, it's all been 'fiddled with' – iPads, phones, the oven, the doorbell, an ancient heater trolley, aircon controller or the backwards rotating fans. Our lessons go in one ear and out the other. My parents are like broken electrical items themselves, and each visit is like explaining who you are to someone who's just woken up from a coma.

'Don't you remember? I showed you how to do this last time. You just click the back button and that takes you back to Netflix.'

I'm not sure if I am talking to my parents or the children some days. Our conversations are so similar.

'It looks like it will go really fast. I really want it.' They are back to the convertible. The voice is deep, so I know it's my dad this time.

'Why?'

'We just want one. Well, your mother wants one.'

'Right.' I wonder how to approach the topic without telling them what to do.

'I want one too, and I also want to live in a mansion in Beverly Hills, but that doesn't mean I'm going to do it.'

'John, can you give it a once-over?' They hand my husband the address of someone they have dealt with online.

'Is it legit? It seems a bit too cheap to be true.'

'Of course it's legit. His name is double-barrelled!'

My mum thinks anyone who has a hyphenated surname or buys vegetables in packets 'already cut up' is legit.

'You shouldn't buy it.' He looks at the listing on Mum's iPad screen. 'It's a piece of shit and Mr Braxton-Smith looks like he wants to kill me in his profile pic.'

'Well, we've already had our offer accepted. It can't be a piece of shit. It's a convertible.'

'Does the roof even work?'

'I don't know. I didn't ask. It doesn't rain here much anyway. It will be fine.'

My husband and I know the drill. Our opinions on their hasty decision to buy an old banger off Marketplace are as pointless as an inflatable dartboard. Once Mum has decided, all practical trains of thought crash into the side of a mountain. Her 'I want it now' Veruca Salt brain means my husband will now spend the next six months trying to find used car parts for crappy convertible Saabs, fixing oil leaks, and being called upon to pick-up two soggy grey-haired speed demons from the side of the road when the roof, and the car, break down.

Mum sees our unconvinced expressions and changes the subject.

'Dad and I are going on a cruise. There's a deal on. Up to Vanuatu and back. You don't even have to get off the boat. Leaving next Friday. We even get a three hundred dollar booze voucher.'

'Really? That sounds like a bargain. They'll probably throw in a bout of Covid and influenza A for an extra fifty dollars … just like last time.'

My parents had boarded a boat last year as fit as fiddles and came off looking like they had been dragged keelhaul over spiky barnacles and left in the sun for four days to die. Their skin was leathery and they were limping like pirates. Illness had ravaged the boat and they had been bedridden from day two, booze vouchers still intact and no invite to the captain's table in sight.

Every time my parents go on a cruise – or buy anything from Facebook Marketplace – I have visions of them being returned to me in body bags.

'Well, it's booked. Lyn's coming too.'

Most of the time I just sit back and watch my mum and dad get on with it. I can't tell them what to do, and when I do they don't listen. I've decided as I have gotten older just to soak up all the good bits. I'm just glad to have them and happy that they still have all their faculties.

My grandad, William, had Alzheimer's disease when he was their age. I was too young to understand his symptoms and just thought he enjoyed asking me eighteen times if I liked tinned spaghetti hoops. I think his illness must have scared my parents, and watching him deteriorate made them very aware of ageing and what could happen if they ever get unwell.

'Roger, if I get Alzheimer's and I'm having a moment of lucidity, just say to me, "You've got Alzheimer's, Maureen" and give me a pill so I can end it,' Mum said one morning. 'I don't want anyone to have to look after me, I'd rather just go.'

Without hesitation my dad looked at her and said, 'You've got Alzheimer's, Maureen.'

We all laughed out loud and watched as Mum's copy of *The Satanic Verses* flew across the room and hit Dad so hard it knocked his glasses off.

Now it's my turn to feel a little scared. Some days, I can't imagine my parents not being here, popping open bottles of bubbly, and others, I'm wondering if throwing a Kindle at their heads would have the same effect as a Salman Rushdie novel. My parents have not become like Grandad William, gentle and forgetful, or like the sweet old people you see in 1980s sitcoms – knitting in a rocking chair, reading gardening magazines, bumbling around talking about bus timetables – they've become opinionated and immune to what anyone else thinks. A lethal combination.

I spend visits ducking under pointed comments about the #MeToo movement like, 'We all had our bums pinched in my day' and sidestepping statements about female football commentators. ('What's this woman doing? Women know nothing about football.') My dad thinks 'being woke' is when the bin truck comes early every Tuesday morning.

If gender, politics or religion come up in conversation, I bolt towards the garage and stay there until the kettle boils and the discussion has moved on to digestive biscuits. (Apparently the Woolies ones best survive 'a heavy dunking'.)

Trying to convince my eighty-five-year-old father that women play football now is as difficult as getting him down from that ladder we keep telling him not to climb.

No matter how opinionated or set in their ways, my parents are fit. Mentally and physically. They walk every day. They dance. Dad goes to French classes, Mum hosts morning teas. They're on their feet, either laying a table for dinner guests, standing at the stove cooking, or leaning down to slide plates into the dishwasher. They have the first joke, the last laugh and party harder than a club promoter on a Miami beach. I have never once heard my dad say, 'I'm tired.' Those two words are not in his vocabulary. He goes to bed after everyone else and wakes up with the tweeting birds. He's always busy, making tea or fiddling with the hose.

'You should go to bed, Dad.'

'No, I'm going to stay up and watch the game.'

'But it's eleven.'

'I'm all right.'

An hour later, the whole house is awoken by what sounds like a donkey giving birth.

Dad sits, head dropped back, chin lit up by the match playing out on the TV, fingers still hold the handle of a cup, balanced on the arm of the couch, snoring so loudly the walls shake.

When I get up in the morning, he's already in the kitchen, freshly shaved, making toast and moaning about immigration. Perhaps all the cheap sparkling wine my parents drank over the years has preserved them, soused their bodies and minds so well that they'll never deteriorate and live forever. Well, at least that's my hope. I can't imagine life without these two overly opinionated pickles.

Mum is staring at the iPad screen. Long painted nails *tap-tap* as she attempts to swipe up and close a page, nothing quite hooking on to her fingertip. I think about showing her, again, but it's like talking to a sponge with eyes, soaking up the information only for it to be squeezed out the moment I stop talking. I will wait until tea-time ... when she asks me again.

This is where I am – midlife, menopause nibbling away at my temperament, my own parents needing more support and my children looking to me for answers. I am stuck between two slowly amalgamating lands. One side learning, the other side wondering what they came into the room for. It's a place most mums get to. Hormones, responsibility, love and disappointment. All mixed up together. Part of my challenge to be a better mum is to be happy where I am. Enjoy everyone while they are still here and healthy. But sometimes life provides situations that are completely out of your control, and all you can do is hope to survive …

Gasping for Air

June

We are in a campervan, on a road trip in Perth, when the worst day of our lives unfolds.

'His lips are blue.'

'He's not breathing.'

After a picnic on a quiet beach, the kids get a lolly each as a treat. I thought nothing of it. I hand them the packet and strap them into their car seats. I get in the front seat, John starts the engine and we pull away.

The next sound is not a sound any mother should ever hear. The sound of their child unable to get air into their lungs.

I turn around to see Fred, mouth wide open, gasping for air.

'STOP THE CAR!

I undo my seatbelt and lurch into the back to undo his seatbelt, and I pull him upwards into my arms.

'He's choking, John.'

I turn him upside down, hit his back, do a Heimlich manoeuvre, but nothing comes out. John pulls up the handbrake and climbs into the back of the campervan.

I'm thumping Fred's back, but his body is floppy, hanging over my forearms. Lifeless like a rag doll.

'He can't breathe. It's not working.'

'Give him to me.'

Our eyes meet as I hand him over.

We both know our son is dying.

'Run out onto the street and shout for help. Run, go now!'

I watch my husband fold Fred's limp little body over his lap and bang his back. I don't look for my phone. No time. I am moving towards the door. I can't reach the handle quick enough.

I burst through the side door of the van into the sunlight and find myself on an empty street in the town of Geraldton. Noise is coming from me, but it isn't talking or shouting. A rough, rasping cry for help heaves its way up and out of my mouth.

'HELP! Please, someone help us.'

A car approaches. I run into its path, waving my arms above my head.

'Call an ambulance, please, our son is choking, we need help.'

The young boy nods and taps his fingers on his phone.

George is behind me now.

'What's happening, Mum. Is he dying? Is Fred dying?'

I get down on my knees and pull him down with me. I hold his shoulders tight and look him in the eye.

'I don't know, sweetheart. I don't know what's happening right now. Go and sit with your sister. An ambulance is coming.'

I see John in the background. His face pale. Fred's floppy body.

I'm not sure how long I kneel there. On the hard tarmac watching my son not come back to life. Maybe one second or five minutes. I hear people around me. I look down and see feet close by. Someone has an arm around me saying, 'It's going to be okay. The ambulance is on its way.'

All I can think is, *I am that mother now. The one whose child died. The one who has never been the same again. My life is over. My son is dying and there is nothing I can do.*

I know this is the point that everything changes.

I squeeze my eyes shut for a moment, trying to push away what's happening around me. Images of Fred flood my mind. I had made him laugh in the shower at the campsite that morning.

'Dat dickles, Mummy!'

'Arms up,' I said. 'Let's do your pits.' He turned like a ballerina in a jewellery box as I sprayed warm water over him to wash off the bubbles. As I rubbed shampoo into his hair, I slid two hands up the side of his head to make a mohawk. 'What a cool boy!'

He grinned up at me. 'I'm Mummy's cool boy.'

When we finished, I wrapped him up in a soft blue towel and gave him a rub. 'That's better, all clean. Now, let's go and find the others.'

We turned to leave, and his little hand snuck into mine. Neither of us spoke. I squeezed it as if to say, 'I love you so much it hurts!' He squeezed back and with the towel dragging along the dusty pathway behind us, we made our way back to the van.

More voices.

Fred being carried onto the side of the road.

All I see are flashes. Snippets of what is going on. I am too scared to look. Two men, builders in high-vis and dirty boots, take charge. They see John is losing hope.

'He's not breathing.'

One of the men puts his thumb and forefinger in my son's mouth, trying to open his airway. A last resort, a final attempt at bringing him back to me. More people, a circle around us. My son in the middle, surrounded by the hope of strangers. Me on the periphery not knowing what lies ahead. I look away. The wall I have built is crumbling around me. My one job as a mum, to keep my children safe, is sliding away.

A warm gust of wind, a change in the atmosphere. Through a forest of legs, a face turns towards me. The man kneeling next to my son is looking at me, fierce blue eyes looking directly at me.

'He's breathing.'

I fall forward onto my hands and begin to cry. I breathe again too.

I hear the siren.

In that moment, when the air fills both our lungs, I understand love. I understand its depth and its weight.

Fred did not die that day.

He came back.

*

We spend a night in Geraldton hospital. Just me and Fred. I lie in the bed next to him. He sleeps for about twelve hours, not even waking when the nurse does his blood pressure.

'He's been through a big trauma. You might find he is sleepy for a few days,' says the nurse as she undoes the velcro armband.

It's dark on the ward. There are other people in the beds around us. Some watching TV screens that glow a bright blue colour. A lady with a trolley full of trays delivers food and cups of tea. I don't eat. I just lie there, with pins and needles, holding Fred, knowing that this could have been a very different day, knowing how close I came to being the mother who watched her son die. I hold him all night.

Fred wakes up the next morning, back to his old self. He watches TV and eats a chocolate mousse in bed. The other kids come in to visit and we all sit around chatting, pleased to still be a family of five. The nurses come in and tell us how lucky we are. But I don't feel lucky, I feel sick. After being discharged we go and find the builders who saved Fred's life. We shake their big, dry hands and they lift him up onto their shoulders and we take a photo. I smile with tears in my eyes. I must look relieved, the mother whose son survived, but again, that is not what I'm feeling.

We try to get on with the holiday, but this blackness sits in the pit of my stomach.

'Vicky, just try and concentrate on the positive side. We are all alive.'

But I can't.

I can't be okay.

Back to Therapy

The foreboding doesn't go away. We get back from our trip and I try to get on with life. A menacing fear is sitting on the edge of my existence. But I don't tell anyone. I just do my pretending. I put on a front.

'Yes, it was awful. A parent's worst nightmare. But he's fine, we're all okay now.'

Externally, I take on my husband's 'Let's just get on with it' attitude. I stick a smile on my face and carry on, but the immeasurable fear of nearly losing Fred is changing me. Seeing Fred's colour drain from his face showed me how fragile my children really are.

When I had George, I did worry, all the time. It was the natural doubts of a new mum, stressing about feeding, sleep routines. But with each subsequent child, my worry subsided. I became more confident with motherhood and the thought of them being harmed dissipated. I knew love meant risking loss, but my kids were so alive, so loud, so vibrant, that I never stopped to consider anything else.

Until the incident.

It's haunting me, every single day. My default is set to danger. It's not something anyone can see. You carry on with life with a searing pain, hoping it will just go away.

'I'm not feeling very well, mentally. I'm worrying too much,' I say to John.

'It's okay, Vic. Fred is okay.'

'I know, but what if something else happens?'

His eyes meet mine.

'Go and see someone, talk it out. It will help.'

*

This has happened before in our lives. Me, falling apart. John knows that sometimes I need help undoing what's tangled up in my head.

I head to the local doctor.

'I'm overwhelmed,' I say before my bum even hits the chair.

'What's going on?'

'I'm scared but I don't know why?'

'Has anything happened, Victoria?'

'Yes, something did happen.'

I tell him about Fred.

143

'It's making me paranoid one of them is going to die at any moment.'

I tell him how the worry is playing out. It's the first time I've aired my rather irrational actions in one fell swoop, and when I list the 'adjustments' I've made since Fred choked, I realise I sound like a maniac!

'I taped bits of carpet to sharp table corners and fit foam stoppers to ensure hands don't get slammed in doors. I replaced all the blind cords, moved the beds away from the ceiling fans, banned skateboards, threw away the microwave popcorn and of course any sweets that look about the same width as a larynx. I've tagged all three kids like sea turtles. GPS trackers hang from the zips of their school bags. I cut grapes in half, mash up carrots and squash melon with a bent fork. I crush bags of crisps with my bare hands until they've disintegrated into breadcrumbs. I drive next to them as they ride their bikes home from school. I insist on staying at parties when the invitation says parents can 'drop and go'. Leaflets about rugby league and Aussie rules clubs are hidden in the bin, along with the book club pamphlet ...'

'Go on.'

'I lecture them about the dangers of motorbikes, plug sockets, men with puppies in the boot of their car, snakes in long grass and dogs you don't know. I hover nearby like a drone. Watching their every move. Is that a bit much?'

'Yes. It is a bit,' he says as he taps at his keyboard.

'And I'm checking, always checking. I have to see if they are all breathing okay after they go to bed. My brain is completely preoccupied with the safety of my children. I think I need some help.'

*

My therapy referral appointment letter arrives a few days later.

I drive into town feeling hopeful. Answers.

Callie has blonde curly hair and a soft South African accent; she greets me with a warm handshake and asks me to take a seat.

'So, why are you here?'

'I'm worrying too much. I'm scared one of my children might die at any moment. I've been feeling anxious. I haven't felt this wobbly since my last ever hangover, six years ago. An impending doom sits on my chest from the moment I wake.'

I burst into tears.

'My anxiety hangs around me like a bad smell. I can't shake it off. It's getting worse. Lasting longer, becoming part of me. I'm losing myself to it, losing my confidence. I need to get back to who I was.'

'Well, you've done the right thing coming here, Vic. Tell me all about it.'

Over the following weeks, together, we undo my dread. I'm frazzled after each meeting, but glad to know how I have been feeling is a normal reaction to what I saw. I have underlying trauma since watching my son unable to breathe. That image is sitting just under my skin, sizzling away and sneaking into everything I do. Nearly losing him shook me and it wasn't something that was just going away, it needed time and care.

Callie and I discuss everything: work seeping into parenting, how I worry about others before myself, lack of confidence, friendships, motherhood. We even do a bit of hypnotherapy. I visualise putting all the people who annoy me into the basket of a hot air balloon and then watch them float away. As I wave goodbye from the ground, something clicks inside me, a quiet realisation of who truly matters. I feel good afterwards.

I learn every time I'm there, little titbits to keep me moving forward, tools that help me grow up and slow down. Each week my anxiety lessens.

After ten appointments …

Just like Fred, I come back too.

Then, one night, I get up for some water in the middle of the night. I see a shadow in the hall near Fred's bedroom.

George.

He's standing in the darkness.

'Are you all right, George? I thought you were asleep hours ago. What are you doing?'

'Just checking.'

'Checking what?'

'Just checking that the others are still breathing.'

My heart sinks.

*

I had not thought about anyone else. Stupid really. I had not considered that trauma's creeping tendrils might snag him. I was too busy, up in the air, worrying about my own mental health ... that I forgot to look down.

It's subtle at first. Just the peering around the door, looking each night. Then he starts to ask the same question all the time:

'Where's Fred?'

'I think he just went into the garden to get his football.'

As soon as Fred is not in his eye line, he asks again.

'Where's Fred, Mum? I can't see him.'

'He's on the toilet, George. He is safe.'

*

George's worry escalates over a matter of weeks. If he can't see Fred for more than ten seconds, he goes pale and runs up and down the house shouting his name. He plops directly into a fight-or-flight response, back into the moment he thought he saw his little brother dying.

I do my best.

'He's safe, George. I have an eye on him. Your dad and I will keep him safe. That's our job. We are the parents. It's our role to look after him. Trust us.'

But the trust is gone. He saw us unable to revive Fred, unable to wake him. He saw us pass a limp body over to some strangers on the roadside that day, because we didn't know what to do. George saw that sometimes Mummy and Daddy don't have all the answers. We lost control of the situation and it shifted something in him.

He has to keep Fred safe because maybe we can't.

This fear plays out for George every day. He is stressed. Uncomfortable being around his little brother and sister, scared something bad will happen to them.

'Where's Nell, Mum? Have you seen her?'

I know it's not really anyone's fault that this is happening, but I can't help feeling sad. Sad because he is too young to feel this anxiety and sad because I know how it feels. The only way he knows how to deal with the stress of one of them potentially being in danger is to try and control their every move.

'Nell, stop climbing on the couch.'

'Fred, put the chocolates back in the fridge. You're not allowed them.'

'Muuum. Fred and Nell are not doing as I say.'

'I'm coming,' I say.

One Sunday, we are having a family barbecue at Gympie Terrace and Fred scoots off towards the bandstand. I have an eye on him. I know where he is. But I can see George running towards me, his face as white as snow.

'Mum. I can't see Fred.' He pants. His whole body is shaking.

'It's fine. I can see him. You must stop worrying, George. I am his mum and I will protect him.'

George sits down on a camping chair and starts sobbing.

'You can't protect him, Mum. None of us can. He is going to die and there is nothing we can do.'

'But it's safe here, George.'

'It's not safe, Mum, there is a main road there.' He points. 'And the river is there.' He points in the other direction.

I thought we were all having a nice day out but it turns out that George is in a panic-filled nightmare. How could I have not noticed it had got so bad?

'Why are you so worried, George?'

His head is bowed, chin touching his Vans T-shirt.

'Nobody saw what I saw, Mum. Nobody knows how I feel.'

I turn and look at my husband and we share a knowing look. The same one we had in the campervan that day. We have no idea what to do.

'Would you like to talk to someone about it, George, to someone who might be able to help?'

'Yes.'

Kneeling with my hands on his shoulders, I see a boy in pain. I wish I had the answers, but I don't. I give him a big squeeze and I tell him it's going to be okay.

That afternoon, we book our little boy into therapy. When I drop him off for the first session a week later and watch him walk towards the big double doors, a lump appears in my throat.

I have never, ever, been so proud.

Grated Expectations

I can hear the disturbing rattle of a little hand in the cutlery drawer.

'Mum, Fred has a skewer,' George says in a monotone voice.

Fred's kamikaze lifestyle is not pushing George over the edge for once. Progress. George is slowly getting better. We don't talk too much about what goes on in the sessions. I don't badger him for once. I trust the process and take a step back. It's what he needs – and what I need too.

'Tell him to put the skewer down. I'm coming.'

I get up, pull a T-shirt on and head in the direction of the potential impaling.

The metal stick is prised from a tight hold and threats about 'going in to speak to teachers' bounce off the walls. Then I get the lunches ready.

'Right you lovely lot, what do you want in your lunchboxes today? Foie gras? Some caviar perhaps? Maybe a sirloin steak with pepper sauce and a crème brûleé for dessert?'

'Have we got cheese?' asks Nell who is hovering nearby, watching my every move.

'Yes, I have a block of your finest Somerset cheddar in the fridge. Cheese and Vegemite it is!'

'I don't like sliced cheese, Mum.'

'Well, you liked it yesterday.'

'I like grated cheese, the crusts off and the bread cut into triangles and not squares.'

'Okay, darling,' I seethe.

'And please don't put strawberries in with the crisps. It makes them go all soggy.'

'Yes, your majesty. Is there any particular water you would like in your *bouteille* today? Still? Sparkling, a twist of lime perhaps?'

'Stop it, Mum.'

I make holes in the bread as I try to spread cold butter, then scrabble around in the top drawer to find a serrated knife that won't abolish the edges of her flawless sarnie. I cut it into triangles. Once it's quartered, I pop it in the chosen spot. One compartment complete.

The bento lunchboxes I stupidly chose have words printed on the bottom of each snug cubicle. There's Fruit, Dairy, Vegetable, Protein and Grain. For some weird reason I, being the good mummy that I pretend to be, abide by the rules of the box as if my life depends on it.

When the demands of the box get too much, I find a 'Bento Mom' on Instagram. I scroll through videos of culinary goddesses with beach curls and frilly aprons preparing kid food as if it was for a five-star degustation. I watch a clip in which the mum uses edible markers to draw funny faces on sandwiches. (The only edible markers in my house were the wax crayons my five-year-old devoured, resulting in multicoloured excrement for three days.) Then I watch a red-lipped homebody with perfect nails construct a white rabbit out of a boiled egg, turn pretzels into butterfly wings and push green-pea noses onto ham faces.

Where do these women find the time? I don't have time to put underwear on, let alone carve names on cucumbers. I bet when the camera is off, she shoves a bruised banana and cheese roll in a paper bag like the rest of the tired mum population, but still, I can't help feeling the pressure. At a recent playdate, a proud Bento Box Mum had unfolded an incredible tiered box of wholesome delights. There are swirls of hummus, cherry tomatoes on toothpicks that looked like caterpillars and indecipherable nut mixes that resembled bird food and rodent droppings.

'Did you bring some snacks, Vic?'

'Yes.' I produce an apple, a packet of Twisties and a half-eaten sushi roll.

She avoided me for the rest of the morning and I overheard her say the words 'I'm not joking, Cheese Twisties!' to one of the other mums.

The truth is, I do make healthy food sometimes, but my kids don't eat it.

'Come on, kids. Food is one of life's biggest pleasures. Try it.'

'Yuck!'

'It's not Oysters Kilpatrick for god's sake, it's a sweet potato.'

Nell pukes into her own mouth. Fred spits it on the floor and George goes pale as he stares at it on the end of his fork.

'Right, well, you'll have to eat a bit of the salad then and we are not leaving the table until you've all eaten some vegetables.'

This food battle is something I do once a month. My hormones make me mean and unforgiving. I'm like a prison guard, standing over them watching their every move, making sure something goes in.

'Have I had enough, Mummy? Can I leave the table now?' George begs.

'One more bit of carrot and you're done.'

'Now?'

'Yep, you're done. Good work, George.'

I think my first child got the VIP service. George was soaked in kombucha, homemade organic mash and wholemeal rice crackers. I had more time with him, I made interesting meals. He never had to share. He could have a packet of Grain Waves to himself back then, no hands snatching at his snack. Then the second kid came along, and the packets got halved. The food effort was less because there were more bums to wipe. By the time the third bottomless pit arrived, making creative lunchboxes became as important as remembering to return a library book on time. With each child I realised if they were eating a few bites of fruit and a couple of veggies each day, then that was okay.

I push the bento box lid on and my Apple Watch goes *bing* to let me know I've met my exercise goal for the day. I wonder if it's the morning boot camp that has helped me reach my target or grating a kilo of cheese.

When the kids get home from school, I do the usual.

'Hello! What did you do at school today?'

They all say in unison, 'Nuffing.'

'Well, that's lovely, can you get your lunchboxes out of your bags, please?'

I peel off the lids and tip them over into the bin. Healthy food rains down onto a water bill and other waste.

'How come you didn't eat your lunches today?'

'You know we don't eat green stuff, Mum. Anyway, it was Mr Harrison's birthday and the whole school had pizza for lunch.'

*

The next day I pack some rice crackers, a cheese roll, fruit roll-ups, some grapes (not impaled with toothpicks) and a shop-bought chocolate chip muffin. No grains, pulses or super salad wraps in sight.

'What happened to the bento boxes?' asks John when he sees me wrapping the cheese roll in foil.

'They were too demanding. I couldn't fulfil their needs. Bento boxes make me feel like a bad mother!'

'Good idea. I hate them too. By the way, why was there sliced cheese in my sandwich today? You know I prefer grated.'

I go to hit him with a wooden spoon, but he runs away laughing.

A Three-legged Race

August

I pop the invitations to *Nell's Princess Party* into the little pockets hanging on her classroom door. When her friends see the pink paper poking out, they all squeal with delight. They know it's going to be epic.

I'm good at throwing kids' parties. Exactly one hour and thirty minutes of chaos. Fun with a time limit. Perfect. I'm in control and I can avoid chatting with parents because I'm busy doing jobs. I've put up bunting, filled tables with snacks and blown up a hundred gold balloons. By the time the girls arrive, my house looks like a fun fair.

'Hi, you're welcome to stay, or you can just pop back and grab her later,' I tell the parents. 'Any allergies?'

It goes well. There's a dance-off, a demolished cupcake tower, a treasure hunt and a 'pin the wand on the fairy' game. As they leave, I hand out party bags containing yo-yos, sherbet straws and lip balm. The kids trundle out the gate, holding hands with their mummies, saying, 'That was the best party ever.'

Job done.

But, when the party is out of the safe confines of my own home, somehow the 'legendary party mum' gets sucked up a curly straw leaving 'absolutely no personality mum' in her wake. I become a polite, tiptoeing numbnut, a mum whose anecdotes are about as interesting as a plank of wood. I know a kids' party could be a great place for me to make some more new friends, but being confronted with so many people I don't know in one place makes me self-aware. To avoid morphing into this socially inept dullard, I've had to become a dropper-offer. A 'shove the kid out of the car and wheel spin out of the driveway' sort of mum. Yet again, not the mum I thought I would be.

'Please come this time, all the other mums are staying. It's a sports theme. We're going to play lots of games, and you can join in,' pleads Nell.

She is standing at the bathroom mirror putting on my mascara, getting ready for her friend's eighth birthday party. It's at the local park.

'Oh Nellie, you know I hate going to kids' parties where I don't know anyone.'

'Just this once and I'll never make you go again.'

I have a flashback to my first ever Sunny Days Parenting class all those months ago.

Remember why you wanted to be a mum in the first place, Vic.

'Okay, Nell. I'll come. But I'm not doing the three-legged race.'

I walk towards the park carrying a plate of fairy bread, and Nell has a little gift bag hooked over her wrist with a plastic crown inside.

'I think they're going to beat each other today, Mum.'

'BEAT EACH OTHER?'

'Yes, I don't want anyone to get beaten.'

I was worried for a second until I realised, she didn't mean that kind of beating.

'Oh, you mean they are going to have running races?'

'Yes.'

'Don't worry,' I said. 'It's not winning that's important, it's the taking part.'

'I know, I just don't want to race against my friends. If I win, they might not want to be friends anymore.'

'Gosh Nellie, you are so smart.'

She spins on her sparkly red heels and totters off towards the bunting draped around the barbecue pavilions.

I hold back. Giving myself a moment of tranquillity before I enter the carnage. I can see from my position (hiding behind the public toilets) that there is a piñata hanging from a tree, plastic plates filled with sweets on pink tablecloths, cartons of juice piled up in an eskie and a baby with a baggy nappy bumbling around, chewing on a piece of bark. Girls in tutus and boys in soccer shirts are chasing bubbles, and a dad at the barbecue turns sausages with tongs.

I inhale and head over.

I do a few pathetic waves at people I recognise and dawdle around like a spare part until the piñata begins. Children start slamming a baseball bat into the paper camel until its insides burst out. Watching our offspring turn into violent barbarians distracts us all from the awkwardness for a moment.

*

The parties I attended as a kid were not like the ones in Australia. They weren't outdoors in gardens, ovals and playgrounds with slides so hot they burnt a layer of skin off your arse. They were usually held on rainy days in someone's lounge with grandparents sitting on dining room chairs and a slightly creepy magician who tried to get children to sit on his knee for a bit too long. I'm not sure what sort of training you needed to become a children's entertainer back then? Perhaps just a criminal record, a balloon-twisting diploma and a history of hiding animals in your trousers. Whatever it was, they were always terrible and their jokes worse than the ones you get in Christmas crackers.

'Hello! I'm Ian, the fish from Wokingham Wizards.' He fanned a pack of cards and held them out to me. Instead of a black top hat, he wore what I can only describe as a 'fish helmet'.

'Now pick a cod, any cod.' He smiled.

His entire career was based on that one joke. It *was* funny, but unfortunately the highlight of the show.

'Right, lie down kids.'

We obeyed the fish man.

'It's time for the sleeping mackerel competition.'

Me and my mates laid on our fronts, dust from the shagpile making our noses twitch. And for twenty minutes, didn't move or speak. (Yes, I have used it since.) The prize was a balloon shaped like a massive penis.

'This is Mr Snaky,' he said as he handed it over. I remember going up to my mum, who stood on the periphery with a concerned expression.

'Look what I won, Mummy!'

'Don't touch it, Victoria. Put it down. And don't bob on his knee again.'

The finale was an extremely crap attempt at ventriloquism in which a fluffy bunny appeared from a hat waving a little black wand with white tips. The so called 'magician' proceeded to talk out of the side of his mouth.

'Hello derr chill-den, I'm Fumper. And I am 'ere to show you a few twicks.'

There was lots of smacking the wand down, tapping it on cups that housed small fluffy balls, and some awkward fumbling and clanging as metal hoops dropped to the floor. As he performed, my eyes drifted to a coffin-shaped box behind him, which I presumed was for the encore. Mum came over and yanked me away from my friends.

'Come on, let's go.' I grabbed my party bag full of flumps, candy necklaces and a jelly finger-puppet monster. 'I don't want you watching someone get sawn in two. You already have a half-sister.'

Whenever I had a birthday party at home, Mum didn't hire any entertainment, we just played games. All of which risked personal injury.

Musical chairs – usually ended in someone being winded.

Musical statues – where the head bangers and over-energetic robot dancers knocked into each other and got concussions. (This actually gained more high fives than the cheaters doing 'small dancing'.)

Murder in the dark – select and blindfold one person to be the 'murderer child' everyone else hides. The 'murderer child' then has to spend twenty minutes in pitch black, bumping shins into coffee tables and absolutely shitting themselves.

Pin the tail on the donkey – my dad liked to turn this one up a bit for his own amusement. He spun each child around ten times and shouted directions at them.

'Left a bit. Right a bit. Now pin!'

We all had to lurch out of the way as a dizzy child with arms out in front staggered forward, bearing a sharp brass drawing pin.

By the time my birthday party was over, the cake eaten (a Swiss roll train from the *Watkins Cook Book* that everyone got for Christmas in 1978) and a round of the 'Birthday Bumps' (where the birthday girl was used like a double Dutch skipping rope and lucky to get out without a major back injury), everyone went home. And I fell asleep on the sofa, exhausted after overdosing on sherbet flying saucers.

As I got older my parties became a bit more innovative. I had a punk party once. All the kids arrived with green mohawks, safety pins through clothes and aggressive expressions. We played 'pass the parcel' and danced around the stereo singing along to the Sex Pistols. It was brilliant.

*

The party that is laid out before me isn't like that. It is all squashy and fluffy in comparison. Some of the kids are having running races and some are helping themselves to bowls of popcorn. I sense if I suggest we stick on some punk classics, pogo around the war memorial and choose a 'murderer child', it wouldn't go down well.

I mosey over, steal a big triangle of watermelon from a platter and pretend to be an introvert for as long as humanly possible.

The afternoon wears on. A few times I daydream that Ian the fish magician will appear and wave his crappy wand.

'I galdy piggelty wiggerly woo. I will disappear you! Taaaaa daaaaaa!'

But magic isn't real, and Ian the fish magician is probably in prison. Instead of vanishing in a puff of smoke, I sit on a picnic rug remembering why I used to drink buckets of booze and fall asleep in wheelbarrows. Situations like this were much easier after a few drinks.

But, for Nellie, I get on with it. I smile as they sing, 'For she's a jolly good fellow'. Get a band-aid out when Scarlett hits her chin on the drinking tap and let out a strange laugh when the 'head dad' makes a hilarious quip about 'leaving all the women to do the washing-up'. Luckily for him, I am immune to narrow-minded remarks like this. There is nothing more futile than arguing with extremely stupid people.

Nellie comes over and I tell her to grab her shoes.

'We're going in a bit. We've got to take George to wakeboarding,' I say with a knot in my stomach, knowing I have gone against my no-lying rule.

'But we're playing, Mummy. We are just about to make some necklaces.'

She's disappointed because her afternoon is very different from mine. I am wading through clumsiness in my own self-imposed social nightmare and she's having the time of her life, in her element, chasing her friends and playing games.

The boys have run off to climb on the play equipment and the girls are sitting in the shade, under a big oak tree nearby. One of the girls in the group is tipping over a box of beads. She pulls string from a ziplock bag and hands reach in to grab the glittery ones that are pooling in a dent on the mat. They sit in a circle and begin making necklaces, pausing occasionally to hold their creations against one another's necks.

'Do you like it? You can have it when I'm finished.'

They giggle. It's so sweet and innocent. I suddenly feel selfish.

I realise then that the whole time I have been at the party I have been thinking about myself. I've made a child's outing to a birthday party about me! Worrying about my own connection with people, judging everyone and secretly hoping for a wapple. How silly of me. How self-centred. I was focusing on whether I was enjoying myself rather than whether Nell was.

Suddenly a feeling of embarrassment envelops my body. Luckily no one is close enough to see me blush at my own stupid behaviour.

I take a deep inhale and … I give myself over. The only trick left up my sleeve is to make up for it and ensure Nell has the best day ever.

'Okay, we can stay for a bit.'

I sit back down and decide to try. I swivel around to one of the mums and say, 'Hi, I'm Vic. Which one's yours?'

She points out her daughter who is braiding Nell's hair and adding pink beads to the ends.

'That's her. They're playing nicely. Perhaps we could organise a playdate sometime?'

'Errr …' I shake my head as if a bee has flown in my ear. I probably look batshit crazy, but I hope the rapid movement jolts my brain and resets my automatic response.

It works.

'Yes, that would be lovely.'

We chat for an hour and with my guard down at last, I let her in, and the awkwardness dissipates. We sit on a bench in the sunshine and share some stories about our girls. Before it's time to go, I tell her about what Nell had said before the party started.

'My Nellie, she's a funny one. She didn't want to race anyone today, in case she won. She feared upsetting the other kids.'

The mum leans against my shoulder and whispers, 'Let her run. Let her win.' She glares at 'head dad' over by the barbecue. 'Otherwise, she'll end up doing the dishes for absolute fuckwits like him!'

I laugh so hard I nearly piss myself.

'Right,' my new mummy friend gets up and turns to me. 'It's time for the three-legged race. Shall we do it together?'

'Yes, let's.'

At the starting line, I lean over to tie my leg to hers with a bit of rope and see an upside-down Nell through the gap in my legs.

Our eyes lock and a big proud smile fills her face.

And right then … I remember why I wanted to be a mum.

The F**king Park

It's Saturday. John has gone to help my parents put up a fence, there are no sports games on and I have not made any plans. Major mumming error. As all mums know, doing nothing on a Saturday is impossible.

Before I've even had a coffee, they are hanging off me like rotting fruit, asking questions.

'Can I go to the shops and buy a three thousand dollar mountain bike today?'

'No.'

'Can we all go to Australia Zoo today?'

'No.'

'Can I go to Gone Bonkers and spend my money on slime?'

'No.'

'Let's make lemonade and sit on the road and sell it to passers-by.'

'No.'

My kids think I have thousands of dollars at my disposal and that I excrete enough fresh lemons to make lemonade.

'Guys, can't we just chill? Just stay home and relax?'

'Relaxing is boring. Let's go to the park.'

Urgh. I spent a whole day there for Nell's friend's birthday last weekend. I'm not sure nice, accommodating mummy can hack it again today.

But our local park *is* the easiest option.

'Okay' I sigh. 'Park it is.'

I pack a bag with some packets of chips, a picnic rug, suncream and water bottles as the kids get their shoes on. I look out of the kitchen window. Big black clouds hover above but it looks like the rain will hold off for a while, so we leave the car at home and head towards the park with our little dog, Sandy, taking the lead.

I like walking to the park. I hang back, watching, as two kids on scooters and one on a skateboard zoom up ahead. I pass my favourite gum tree with huge curling leaves, have a nose at all the new builds popping up along the street and say hello to a border collie yapping at a wire fence.

When we arrive, I dump the bag and look around. It's empty apart from a bush turkey pecking at a discarded box of Jatz crackers.

Here I am. At the bloody park again.

I plonk myself down on a wet bench and do the unthinkable, the most terrible, shameful act a mother can do.

169

I look at my phone.

I search for Thai curry recipes, book to get my eyebrows done and write a few witty comments under Facebook posts. My phone helps me escape from the park.

I've been going to the same park for eleven years. Parks are not like computer games, they don't get regular updates, there are no cheats or new levels. Parks seem to stay the same forever.

I didn't like parks much as a kid either. My mum always told my sister and I the same story when we used to walk to our local park. Her brother had stood on the top of the slide, calling to his little sister Pat, who was sitting on the asphalt below. My mum said, 'I saw the rock flying through the air and then … the blood fountain. It was awful!' The rock had landed on her little sister's head. My mum, being the oldest, had to pick up her baby sister, hold her cardigan sleeve on the wound and carry her to Auntie Rose's house where she got sewn up by Doctor Morrison. I have never been able to dislodge the image of a blood fountain from my head. So I developed an ingrained fear of parks. I felt unsafe in them, and was on the lookout for orbiting missiles from that day onwards.

It was probably a good thing.

Kids' parks in England in the early 1980s were like battlegrounds. No health and safety visits from the council back then. As a sprog, I went to a park near Reading, the town in which I grew up for the first seven years of my life. Most parks in England aren't enticing due to relentless drizzle and groups of hooded teenagers who lurk in cubby houses smoking spliffs, flicking matches at each other and gobbing onto the asphalt. My local park was no exception. It was always wet, rain dribbled down the slide into a brown puddle at the bottom and two girls with hair pulled back in tight buns used to shout comments at me as I slipped from the monkey bars.

'Wot yer mum dressed ya like that for, ya div? Scared of losin' ya fakin mittens, are ya? Twat!'

They had a point. My mum had dressed me in a duffle coat like Paddington Bear and it had a string running across my back, from one hand to the other, each end attached to a woollen mitten. It was a bit on the nerdy side. But I never lost my gloves.

It wasn't just the local girls who had a screw loose; the equipment did too. There were bolts missing, rusty rivets, wobbly climbing frames, everything there was a threat. The witch's hat spun faster than a Catherine wheel, the rocking horse didn't rock and the swing set was missing a seat on one side while the other had a chain detached. The park was more dangerous than a toddler with a nail gun. Most days, I limped home after getting my leg trapped in the space under the roundabout or I seethed with pain from a nasty chin cut caused by a death-defying leap from the wonky swing.

The flooring wasn't spongy like it is now either. No sandy surface or sprinkling of wooden shavings to lessen the blow. It was solid concrete. If you fell, ambulances were called. But the risk factor added at least a bit of edge to the park experience. The threat of death made it more interesting than staying home and sliding down the banister. Park war wounds were badges of honour at school – and as a bonus, it was much easier to convince Mum to buy a packet of Fruit Pastilles if I had blood leaking out of my knee.

*

I know I'm supposed to say how wonderful it is being here, watching them run and play, and I *was* enthusiastic about it for the first few years. But it didn't last. Now the park is boring, I've been here too much. Pushing swings and asking people about their bedraggled home-schooler is not how I want to spend my days.

I'm still sitting on the bench with my head bowed looking at my phone. I am so distracted by a reel of a man playing two pianos at once that only when a stranger taps me on my shoulder saying, 'Erm excuse me, your kid is running towards the carpark,' do I snap out of my online rabbit hole and back into reality.

'Don't worry, he's fine,' I say, but she's right, he is heading towards the carpark. Fast.

'Heeee won't go farrrr,' I shout behind me as I sprint towards my little fiend. I catch up with him and grab onto his shoulders just as a delivery van backs out of a space next to us.

'Don't do that to me, Fred. You scared Mummy.'

I take his hand and head back to the park, where I slip my phone into my bag.

Within an hour the kids are all covered in muck: some of it is bird shit, some is mud, and I hope some of it is chocolate. Dirt flies off clothes as they get dizzy on what we call 'The Spinny Thing'. They leave trails of filth on the slide and have twigs sticking out of their hair. They remind me of my drinking days, waking up after an all-dayer, covered in a film of sludge only wearing one shoe.

At one point, Nell gets stuck up a tree and George falls on a sharp stick and needs a band-aid just as Fred shouts, 'I neeeeeed a poo, Mum!'

I don't know why kids always need a poo at the park? It must be something to do with the excitement and hanging upside down. So, I spend the next fourteen minutes standing in a piss-soaked cubicle saying, 'Don't touch anything!' and 'Are you done yet?'

'Two more minutes, Mum.'

They always know the exact amount of time it takes.

We wait.

I pull paper from the holder as crinkly as crepe paper and stand near the door folding it over and over. Instead of being annoyed or frustrated, I just look at Fred and think how lucky I am. His funny face, bum in toilet, legs swinging until his underpants fall off onto the grubby floor. Yes, I am standing in a urine-filled plop prison for far longer than anyone would like to, but there is a job to do and I just have to wait it out.

Once Fred has wiped and shorts are pulled back into place, I open the door and light fills the space. We wash our hands in freezing water in the cold metal sink and head back to the colourful equipment with mums bobbing babies up and down in carriers while shoving children's legs over high bars.

I try to parent a bit better for the rest of the morning. Once the phone is away, good, earthy, floaty-dress Mummy comes out to play. I push swings, play shops with mulch pies, and sit on the seesaw, bumping the kids into the sky. We get hot chips for lunch and I even manage a smile when Nell walks over holding something up to show me.

'Look Mummy, I found lots of little balls of mud. Look how cute they are!' she says, all excited.

'Wow Nellie, they are amazing.' I smirk, and she skips back towards the slide … with the dried kangaroo turds cupped inside her little hands.

I feel a big drop of water on my head. Rain moves in, making dark spots on the grey road that runs alongside the park. I call the children and we sit, huddled in the little undercover area waiting for it to pass.

'Can we go home and play on the Switch?'

I pause.

This is exactly where, a few months ago, I would have said yes. I would have seen it as an opportunity for some time off being a mum. The children would have spent the afternoon looking at a screen and I would have sat at my desk writing a podcast episode. We would have ignored each other for the rest of the day.

I'm getting better at recognising when I'm taking the easiest option or when I'm being lazy.

I pause, stopping in my own tracks to remind myself that work is not as important as them. My pausing … and then starting over means the gap between me and the mother I want to be is getting smaller.

'No, let's not finish up for the day yet. Let's do a big walk in the rain? How about we go home, grab the car and head to Ninderry?'

I ignore their groans.

*

The kids all do an amazing job on the hike. Tired legs keep moving until we reach the lookout. We all lean in for a damp selfie, four red faces saying cheese. It's an incredible view, the whole Sunshine Coast, from Caloundra to Noosa, spread out before us. The rain slows and we can see blue skies up ahead.

There are only three arguments on the way home. One over who sits where, one over Crazy Frog or Bruno Mars, and one between Siri and me.

'Hey Siri, can you please give me directions home?'

'Giving you directions to The Homemaker Centre in Maroochydore.'

'No, Siri, directions to home!'

'Mum, you have to say, "Hey Siri" first.'

'Hey Siri, directions to home please!'

'No Mum, you can't say please at the end.'

I take a very deep inhale.

'Hey Siri, directions to home.'

'I have found this on the web about *Game of Thrones*.'

I pause.

Take a moment, Vic. Start again.

But the pause doesn't work every time.

'Hey, Siri.'

'Yes?'

'Please fuck the fuck off.'

Dizzy with Dots and Stars

We had a great weekend, and I noticed George playing a bit more with his siblings on the walk. He's really improving and not asking about Fred as much. There have been no midnight checks for weeks, and if he does get a bit of anxiety I see him practising the box-breathing technique taught to him by the therapist.

'In for four, out for four.'

I'm really impressed.

But this morning, they are back into Monday habits. Moaning about having showers, whining about brushing teeth, grumbling when searching for lost hats … just taking ages to get ready. I teeter on losing my cool. 'I'm not doing this, I'm going for a walk,' I say to John.

These 'rage walks' are a new tactic that help me calm down. I read about them online. A 'venting outing' or 'rage hike' is a cathartic way to help process intense emotions. As soon as I feel the anger bubbling, I stick my trainers on and basically … leave. John has to pick up where I left off, but it is better than a slanging match about Jake Paul or another daft influencer. The more parenting tactics I have in my toolbox, the better.

I bumped into one of the other Sunny Days mums on my rage walk today. It's been about two months since I last went to a class, and even though I am definitely a tiny bit of a better mum, some of the lessons I learnt are slowly being replaced with bad habits.

'How's it all going? Are you shouting less?' I ask her.

'Yes, I don't shout at all anymore. I don't even do the countdown. I just hold three fingers in the air and they all know what it means.'

I'm awestruck, and to feel better, I decide she is lying.

'How are your three going?' she asks.

'Fred gets it, but the other two are over it. I wish I had started it when they were younger.'

'Try adding a rewards chart for the older ones. I think they need to know they're getting something for being good.'

'Okay. Good idea. Thanks.'

I head to Kmart that afternoon and find a magnetic whiteboard chart with columns for days of the week running along the top and chores down the side. I stick it on the fridge and gather everyone for a family meeting.

'Right, there is a new system in the house. If you all get ready for school on time and there are no quarrels about socks, you will get a prize or some money in your jar at the end of the week.'

'How much money?'

'Five bucks.'

'Is that it?'

'If you moan, I won't give you anything. There is a star for each day of the week, and if you reach five stars you will get your reward. Is that okay with everyone?'

'Yeah.' It's said in a 'I know we don't have a choice' tone.

I had tried this rewards technique before. When George was little, he decided to refrain from going for a number two for about three weeks. As a 'constipation relief incentive' I placed a plastic Buzz Lightyear on top of the door so he could see it but not reach it from the toilet and said, 'If you do a poo, you can have it.'

He sat on the bog for twenty-five minutes, looking up at the toy, as his face turned as red as a beetroot.

Job done.

I find getting the kids ready for school about as painful as expelling a stubborn stool, so it's time to give it another go.

Day one is great. My three little angels stick a star to their column.

Day two is okay. My three hidden hairbrush hooligans are given half a star each.

Day three?

Well, the chart is in the bin, there are star stickers on all the light switches, playdates are cancelled, the pot money has been stolen, Santa Claus has been contacted about behaviour and there are three new additions to his naughty list.

My attempt at untroublesome mornings has scarpered by day three.

But it's not just the kids who are unmanageable.

I am too.

*

I have a calendar on my phone. It looks a bit like the rewards chart. When you add 'an event' (sounds exciting, like a masked ball; it is not), a small dot appears on that day. These little markings look quite pretty, whimsical almost, like petals scattered upon my day by magical fairies. Unfortunately, the dots don't offer gift ideas or tell me how well I've done. They're only announcements of plans that have fallen through. They are there to remind me of promises I can't keep, what is still to do and what I am yet to achieve.

My phone calendar has a dot every single day. They don't represent one event: they represent five events in a twenty-four-hour period.

- Monday – Dog. Speech therapy. School play forms.
  Rotten tangerines back to Coles.

180

- Tuesday – Wart removal. Pay fine. Cancel Stan subscription. Organise meetup.
- Wednesday – Write one chapter. Call prep teacher about shoes.
- Thursday – Boxing. Pay for wakeboarding. Start diet. Call Medicare. Send tiny top back to Shein.
- Friday – Book diabetes blood test, buy nibbles for trivia night. Novelty moustache?

Last weekend at the park was an exception. Most weekends are hectic. I'm either hosting a breakfast for some sober warriors, driving between sports, cooking or going to A&E because one of the life-hoggers has *not* broken their wrist in a skateboarding accident but is making the 'I need an X-ray' face.

When I add appointments, birthday parties and general mum jobs into the diary of doom, I feel organised and superior, like a yuppie with a Filofax. It's only when I check in, each morning in bed with a coffee, that I realise I have added too much and I can't do it all. The dots may look like friendly prompts, but they are black holes. Colourful chasms that are difficult not to fall into. I *am* getting better at separating work from the children. It's all the other 'life stuff' that is clogging up my diary.

I'm a 'yes' person. I turn up. I'm reliable. Annoyingly so. If I say I am going to meet you at a café, I'm there ten minutes early, already having moved seats five times, complained my coffee is not hot enough (twice) and ordered you a cappuccino. I have always had a fear of letting people down, so my own needs get set aside to please others. That's why my diary is full. That's why I often feel like I am scrabbling around between the dots like a rock climber, because I lost a few mates when I gave up being a total piss wreck and I'm trying to desperately hang on to my social life.

I've had so many dots recently that I can't bear to look.

My phone sits on the charger, untouched. Events build up, back to back, like the traffic on the Bruce Highway at rush hour.

I'm so dizzy with dots and stars that I can no longer see a way out.

'My soccer form has to be in today otherwise I can't go.'

'School camp forms are in today, Mum.'

'Have you signed the permission form for the excursion yet?'

Demands crash over me like massive tidal waves. Dealing with the forms from school could fill a whole week. The guilt plane glides past. I want to climb on it and float away.

'I've got too much to do, John. I can't keep up,' I admit to my husband after dinner.

'Have a day off. It's not important. No one cares if you don't go. Just slow down.'

I go to bed, hoping to sleep off the ickiness, then I lie there for six hours (about how long it would take me to answer all my invites) with my eyes wide open, worrying about everything: Why haven't they responded to my text? Is a group of squid called a squad? How do I stop having a shiny forehead? And how much would it cost to buy a yacht and sail around the world, even though I hate yachts and sailing? A head full of rubbish. When I do eventually drift off to sleep, my dreams are so intense I wake up exhausted. (Who knew that working 'the line' in a poo factory and helping Whitney Houston back her caravan into a tiny parking spot could be so tiring?)

I get up the next morning and go to brush my teeth. I look in the mirror and see dark circles under my eyes. I look older. I trudge into the kitchen to make breakfast and the barrage of requests starts all over again.

'Don't forget to book me in for netball.'

'Can you fill in those Year One forms for Fred next year?'

I want to drop to the floor and melt away like the green-faced Wicked Witch of the West.

'Look what you've done! I'm melting, melting.'

My family would be left staring at a pile of clothes on the floor, nothing left except a pair of holey tracksuit bottoms and a *best mum ever* T-shirt.

But my children click their heels and I'm rudely snapped out of my daydream and it's back to the grind, the relentless parenting dot-to-dot.

'I'm feeling a bit depressed,' I say to John as he eats toast crusts from a discarded plate.

'What would make you feel better? Perhaps go and get a massage or something?'

'Nah, I feel beaten up enough already. Maybe I could go and do one of those paint-and-sips?'

But parting with $75 to watch my mates get wasted on chardonnay while I sip on grapefruit cordial and do a rubbish painting of a sea turtle isn't very appealing either.

'I might just go to the shops.'

Going to the shops is a holiday for me. Time alone, staring into windows at items I can't afford, is calming. Just the thought of it makes me feel better.

'Can I borrow your credit card today?'

He looks sad as he hands it over but knows it's far better than another fractured family meeting in which everyone makes promises they can't keep.

Once parked, I take a photo of my spot (B4) and head towards the elevators.

I wander miles of shiny flooring for hours, I buy a cushion, try on a vest top in Target, I go to the Sushi Train, I get my toenails painted bright orange, I ask the eyebrow lady to pluck haphazard hairs out of my chin (there are so many she charges $10 extra), and I spend ages in the bookshop running my fingers along the spines of new releases like the keys of a piano. I like being alone in the shopping centre. It heals me. It's an odd place to repair, but being there without children in tow brings peace.

I'm reminded of how little I get to be alone and how often my life is absorbed into the lives of others.

I wanted a family; it was a conscious choice. I wanted that noisy house full of chaos and laughter, but all of it, all of the time, is utterly overwhelming.

Once the shopping is done, I sit in a little café and order a pot of spicy chai and a muffin. I think about my life. I'm lucky, I know that, but I need a break. I've been charging everyone else up for so long that my battery is low. I need more of this, alone time, me time, time to recuperate and recover from my own life.

It's imperative I get myself together and schedule some time for myself, otherwise everyone else might fall apart.

I decide that drastic measures are in order.

I get out my phone and, for the first time that day, I ignore the dotted diary and instead google 'what are the five best places to run away to?' and a list appears on my cracked screen:

1. For the Thrillseeker – New Zealand
2. For the Beach Bum – Greece
3. For the Spiritual – India
4. For the Nomad – Chile
5. For the Foodie – Italy

Well, I do like food.

Dummies, Bikies
and Babysitting

It's drizzling. I'm sitting at my local café, watching a couple with kids at their ankles ordering baby chinos. I'm alone. A surfer with his wetsuit rolled down to his waist is in the queue holding a pottery mug. The spluttery sound of the coffee machine drowns out conversations. I'm sitting on a wooden bench waiting for my extra-hot soy flat white but I'm going to move inside soon because the rain is getting heavier.

Once in a warm spot in the corner of the café I reach into my bag and get out a travel magazine I bought. I don't tell anyone I've been googling hotels in Italy. I keep it a secret. I go about life with a little bit of hope on the horizon. It may have seemed like a fanciful idea, forgotten about by teatime, but I'm still thinking about it. I'm still considering running away.

A holiday without my children? It doesn't seem like the right thing to do. I can't think of any friends who have done it. There is the occasional husbands' surf trip with the boys, but not many mums with young kids go gallivanting on their lonesome. If you go on a holiday, you go together, that's the rules. It's probably not okay to just run away, but is it running away if I plan on coming back?

Maybe this is what I need – a reset.

I get a glass of cool water from the brass tap. Then I sit for a while and think about my own holidays as a child. The beaches I got to know and love growing up were on our annual summer trips to the south of France. We packed the old caravan, stuffed sleeping bags into the storage spaces under the foam seats, shoved our clothes into overhead cupboards, and rammed towels in cabinets so jars of strawberry jam and bottles of ketchup didn't bang into each other on the journey.

'Righto! Who's coming outside to help me attach the caravan?' Dad would ask.

I'd run onto the driveway, ready to do some competent direction-shouting.

'Back a bit. Forward a bit. Use your wing mirrors. Stop!'

After fifteen attempts and a few 'Come on ya bastard's from Dad, the ball lined up with the tow bar and we were almost ready. Dad handed each kid a yellow felt-tip pen to colour in the headlights of the Citroën. In France, for unknown reasons, car headlights had a yellow tinge and if you didn't adjust yours accordingly you got a fine from the gendarme.

You were supposed to buy a sticky film to place over them, but the felt-tip pens lasted all right. Well, until it rained.

Every year, without fail, before we left to go on our beach holiday, there was a panicked scramble. Mum ran back and forth from the house for forgotten essentials: missing passports, jelly shoes, the bat 'n' ball, a lilo hole-fixing kit and the jar of pickles.

'Don't forget the Branston, Roger!' she shouted at my dad just as he pulled the front door closed. 'They only have those bloody cornichons over there.'

'Cornichons and piss shit!' said my brother from the back seat. (Pschitt! was the name of a local lemonade and we mentioned it as many times as possible each day.)

Dad appeared after a minute and crunched up the driveway, smiling and holding the pickle jar above his head. We all cheered.

When we pulled into Dover, we handed over passports, proudly added our GB sticker to the back window and waited for hours in the long queue. The lowering of the ferry drawbridge signalled it was time to board. One by one, engines started and everyone who was loitering outside their vehicle, having a fag or buying some crisps from the shop, returned and, like animals heading towards the Ark, we snaked towards the mouth of the ship.

The cross-channel ferry always smelt the same: rusty iron and wee, mixed with exhaust fumes. I loved the smell. It meant holidays. We squeezed through the gaps between the cars towards steep metal stairs that led to the passenger deck. Mum made us move quickly.

'Come on kids, we need to get a table in the restaurant before everyone else. Chop chop.'

Mum and Dad went for a posh meal while my siblings and I sat in the cabin eating chips and playing Uno. The cards slipped from the table every time the boat swayed over heaving waves. When they came back from dinner, Dad took us all out of the sliding door onto the blustering deck. We stood together laughing as water drenched our clothes and the boat heaved from side to side. Waves crashed over the railings, and we hooked arms, smiling, wondering if we were all going to die. Mum laughed when we came back in, three drowned rats in desperate need of mugs of a hot drink.

'Come on you lot, take your damp socks off and pop them on the radiator. Hot choccies all round.'

The ferry arrived in France in the middle of the night. It jolted to a stop and a voice came over the Tannoy speakers asking people to return to their cars. I remember Mum kissing my head.

'Victoria, we're here. Grab your teddy and pop your shoes on. We've got to go back to the car.'

Parents carried floppy sleeping children down the metal stairs. Pillows propped up lolling heads. Car doors clicked shut. I heard a *clump* as the car drove onto the metal ramp.

'Steering wheel to the centre of the road, Roger,' Mum whispered as we set off south on the autoroute. I slept for the rest of the journey and woke up just as the boom gate to the campground lifted.

Huge pine tree branches swept dusty pathways that led us to our campsite, and I spent the next two weeks playing Top Trumps on wobbly tables with fold-out legs, crab-hunting with my brother in rock pools, going to the bakery for fresh croissants and eating crêpes à la crème de marrons, a delicious pancake covered with chestnut filling, at a seaside café. We carried our rubber dinghy on our heads to the beach each day, had races down sand dunes and built sandcastles with moats and shell windows. Our days spent together as a family at the beach, running along the shoreline, wearing seaweed moustaches and jumping waves, are my fondest childhood memories.

We only had a couple of slightly traumatising experiences on our beach holidays in France. One time, we saw a Hells Angels member on fire. He stood too close to a gas stove. Mum drove him to hospital and I sat behind him, watching him shiver, his skin blistered and red. I remember being shocked and turning away, only to see twenty Harley-Davidsons cruising behind our old Citroën, chaperoning us to the emergency room. The guy survived. No one messed with us that holiday and we got lots of rides on motorbikes.

Another time, I dropped my dummy in a French toilet. In those days, the toilets in campgrounds in France were just holes in the ground that, when flushed, wet your feet. I didn't know how to squat and toppled over into the damp sewage. I had my dummy in hand and let go before my foot went in the hole.

I remember saying to my mum, 'Get it! Quick Mum!' Unmoving, she stared at me with a sad expression.

'It's gone, Victoria … Forevahhhh.'

I was distraught. Her tone meant dummy time had ended abruptly.

Fair enough.

I *was* eight.

But, dummies and bikies aside, those family holidays to France were diamonds that sparkled in the middle of each and every year. We were left peeling flaky skin from our shoulders, remembering the good times, and spent the following eleven months looking forward to the next time our car bumped down that dusty path to our campsite.

Those memories are why family holidays are so important to me now. They were what bonded us, made us closer. It didn't seem fair to not give my kids the opportunity to make memories such as this … But a need was burning a hole in my gut, even though it didn't feel totally right, I wanted a break.

Apart from a few very rare girls' trips or a weekend in Sydney, this would be the first time I'd left the children. It would be weird not having them near me. John and I hardly used babysitters. Neither of us have ever liked the feeling of being away from the kids.

We tried a babysitting swap arrangement, a 'you have our kids one Friday and we have yours the week after' deal, but after our turn of looking after the kids, my friend got her daughter ready for bed and noticed one of Nell's large tattoo transfers of a bald eagle in full flight, on her daughter's front bottom. It was an awkward phone call, to say the least.

My taking care of other people's children rap sheet doesn't end there. I recently invited five of Nell's best friends to meet us at GameZone, the child gambling hall where slot machines are disguised as penny arcades.

'Don't worry. I'll look after them,' I said confidently to the mums. But I didn't. I lost one. She wandered off and I had to explain to her mother at pick-up why she was crying.

'Lily wandered off for a moment. She was a little upset by the time we found her. I just thought you should know.' (Nell has now experienced a reverse wapple: when you're friends with someone for a long time and then never see them again.)

Oh, and there was also the time I got two toddlers hammered. I was looking after Fred's bestie, Dora. I was finishing a few chores while they played in a big cardboard box. It was quiet for a moment, so I went to check on them and they had vanished. I was beside myself, wandering around the house calling their names. After about five minutes I heard some giggling. I found them hiding under George's bed, surrounded by the wrappers of the posh chocolates I had in the fridge. The alcoholic ones that I couldn't eat. Subsequently I got to read a book on the deck that afternoon while they slept it off.

Of course, grandparents came and went too. I worked out how much childcare was owed before their arrival (an hour for every month of their lives) and my husband and I managed a night away in a hotel about once a year. Apart from that, we don't have any timeouts. We are with our children all the time. It's relentless.

When I moved to Australia I failed to consider the impact such a move would have on getting any time off. My parents didn't move Down Under until the kids were all out of nappies. Most people I knew had relatives living nearby and I felt strange asking people I didn't know that well to take care of what felt like my own beating heart.

Maybe Flat-Nanny could come from England for a week? Help John out. Have some bonding time?

That could work?

*

As I sit in the café, I imagine myself (eighteen, thin and pretty – may as well) sauntering down cobbled Roman lanes in a white, lacy dress, carrying a woven basket filled with bunches of lavender, charming locals with my poor Italian as I ask directions to the 'trattoria'. I could eat where I want, sleep in and do nothing. No one to worry about. A concept as foreign as the country itself.

I mentally bring out the old 'I deserve this' philosophy, a viewpoint I lean upon when doing something I shouldn't, like buying a top I can't afford, squirting whipped cream into my mouth or investing in tasselled cushions from Target. I make an irrational choice without feeling bad about it. I decide I am going to Italy.

I wait a few weeks. Have a chat with Flat-Nanny and tell John. He is slightly pissed off but not enough for me to worry about it. Then I tell the kids.

'Kids, I'm going to Italy!'

'Can we come?'

'Nope. Nanny is coming from England to babysit and Daddy will still be here. I know you're going to be sad, but one day, when you're in your fourties, you'll understand that Mummy needs a break.'

They grunt and turn back to the TV, and I book a ticket.

In the weeks leading up to my departure, I am a bit of a wanker about the whole thing, gloating to friends ('I'm going to Italy!') and saying, 'Ciao!' at the end of phone calls. I buy some espadrilles, a floppy hat and a stripy swimming costume.

But the day before I am due to depart, a wave of anxiety crashes over me. My worst-case scenario mindset creeps up on me as I pack miniature shampoo into my backpack.

What if something happens to them when I'm away?

What if Fred chokes again?

Or I crash the hire car?

I consider writing a note and leaving it in my bedside table, to be read after my untimely death:

Just in case anything happens to me. Just remember how much I love you all.

(Ciao!)

Perhaps ten days on the other side of the world is stretching my umbilical cord uncomfortably far?

'Are you all right?' asks John when he gets home.

'I'm nervous.'

'Why?'

'I don't know? I've travelled so much throughout my life, most of it alone, but this doesn't feel good for some reason. I'm a bit scared.' I burst into tears.

Since having children, my independence has fizzled away like a cheap indoor firework. I had hoped to stay a hippie mum that could breastfeed from a sling as I queued at passport control. I thought the travel spirit was part of me, but Covid, and years of pregnancies and nesting, means I am comfortable. Home is as snug as tracksuit bottoms, and going anywhere beyond the local shops is the equivalent of wearing a polo neck that is three sizes too small. And a recent nightmare family trip to Bali had not helped. Despite the multivitamins, avoiding tap water and not licking any hotel floors, by day three I was lying on cold tiles trying to remember what year it was while failing to predict which orifice would next expel liquid.

'How are you feeling, Mum?'

'Like I've been trampled by a herd of wildebeest and then had my insides fed through a mangle.'

'Are you coming to the beach?'

'No.'

Just as I saw a light at the end of the tunnel, a heaviness enveloped my body. My arms felt as if they were going to drop off and I couldn't taste my nasi goreng. FFS. Covid. I spent another week in bed, crying into my 1000-thread count pillowcase. I didn't want to go anywhere ever again. A weekend in Brisbane and a pub dinner was about as far-flung as this wanderer was willing to travel.

Now, the reality of being 10,000 miles away from my babies fills me with panic. (I briefly wonder if they sell dummies at the airport.)

'You'll be fine. You deserve this,' I say into the bathroom mirror.

I do deserve it, but do they?

John comes in while I'm in the bath.

'Why don't you get someone to come and meet you for a few days, so you don't feel lonely?'

Great idea. I text a mate in the UK and invite her to meet me in Positano. She doesn't need much persuasion and I will have someone to put suncream on my back.

At eleven o'clock that night, John's mum arrives from England. We were like trucks passing on a motorway at night, our paths crossing for a moment.

'Look after my babies. Fred has a sore throat and has his medicine twice a day. Try to get some veggies into them. Good luck,' I say as I hug her.

I put my bags next to the door and do the goodbye tour of their bedrooms. Fred first. Turned on his side, Muddles the beanie dog under one arm, his snuggy blanket clenched in his hand, breathing heavily.

'I love you, Freddie bear, more than anything in the whole wide world.'

George next, covers pushed down, legs spread open like a starfish.

'Be a good boy for Nanny, Georgie.' I kiss his cheek.

'Love you, Mum,' he says in a sleepy voice.

Then Nell. I sit on the side of her bed and she opens her eyes.

'I love you, Mummy.'

'I love you too, Nell. I'll be home before you know it.'

She pulls me in so tight that I can't breathe.
'Time to go to sleep now.'
She sighs and turns over.
Then I head off into the night.

Halfway to *Arrivederci*

I would like to say here that I cry all the way to the airport and the flight is awful and I sit next to a snorer, but that would be a lie.

Going on a flight by myself as a tired mother of three is like a spa day. Even waiting in line at the check-in desk feels like a luxury trip to the Maldives. It's a night flight so the airport is deserted. I whiz through passport control. There are no breakdowns in the airport shop, no demanding of Beanie Boos or expensive colouring books with shite plastic toys stuck on the front. A few shops are still open, so I take my time choosing a book to buy. I pick them up, one by one, read the back cover and put them back. I drift around the airport like a stoned ghost. I have munchies when I feel like it, a croissant and an apple crumble pastry, and I wander around the perfume shop in a haze of Marc Jacobs and Issey Miyake, sniffing my wrist and smiling at the sales lady who knows I am not going to buy any of them.

I sit in a chair and do nothing at all, for ages. I listen as names are called, people late for flights that are destined for countries far away. Then my flight is called.

I shove my bag in the overhead locker, say 'hello' to the man sitting next to me. This is the only time I plan to speak to anyone (apart from saying 'yes' to chicken or fish) and take my aisle seat. I sit and watch movies with no interruptions.

Flights with my kids used to be bedlam. Tears and tantrums all the way to the tarmac. They are only just, since the youngest turned four, getting to the ages where a flight doesn't feel like being locked in a creepy shed with a squirrel on a crack binge. They watch *SpongeBob*, colour in and sleep, knees and elbows pushing up against me as I pull blankets over cold shoulders. It's doable.

As babies it was different. I found flights very stressful, but my worries were dwarfed by the incoming hatred of the other passengers (who, by the way, were snivelling brats once too, but you'd never know). We took George on a twenty-four-hour flight to the UK when he was six months old. Every time he cried, I got stern looks from angry strangers. I could see in their expressions that their peace was ruined by not only my wailing child, but also my own inefficiency as a mother. My husband and I paced the aisles in darkness, George's little feet tapping the heads of sleeping people as we passed. Rocking, soothing, jigging and hoping. *Please be quiet. Please.*

Then the moment he drifted off we expertly manoeuvred him to the clip-in cot. It was like placing a tiny diamond in a ring setting, so much concentration, one false move and it could all be over. I laid the blanket out and John put the precious gem into place. We clipped the seatbelt over his tummy and then removed our hands and stared at one another.

'He's gone.'

Before we had time to do a soft high five, I heard a *ding*.

'We are experiencing some turbulence. Please return to your seats, fasten your seatbelts and refrain from using the toilets. Thank you.'

An air steward came over and asked us to remove the baby from the cot. I leant down and bit the arm rest, which smothered the sound of my internal scream, and then I woke my sleeping baby and started the whole process again. By the time the plane landed both my husband and I resembled the undead: hollow-eyed, slack-jawed, shuffling through the terminal like extras in a budget zombie movie.

As toddlers it was even worse: the screaming got louder and, with punching and biting added to the in-flight entertainment, it meant going back home to visit family in the UK became too hard and, as we reproduced, too expensive.

After watching two movies, I fall asleep. The next sound is the seatbelt *ding* and a soothing Arabic accent asking the cabin crew to prepare for landing.

*

Dark-haired men in white cotton robes walk past in serious conversation. Sandalled toes poke out from underneath. Women float across the ice rink airport floor-tiles in black hijabs. Dubai.

I stop and eat some flatbread at a café to await my connecting flight to Rome. I'm not missing the kids, yet.

And now here I am, halfway to *arrivederci*.

Alone.

And as I sit, nibbling my flatbread and sipping my mint tea, I feel a little part of me come back.

*

The rest of the journey is blissful. Naps and snacks. As I exit the plane down the metal staircase, heat hits my face and I breathe it in.

Outside, a cheery cabbie puts my rucksack in the boot of his car.

'Welcome to Rome. First time?'

I wasn't sure how to answer just in case he decided to rip me off or murder me.

'I've been here before as a kid,' I lie.

'What's your name?'

'Victoria.'

'*Eccellente*. An Italian name. You are like family here Vitoria! I am Fernando.'

I plop in the front and he offers me a sucky sweet.

'Is that drugs?' I joke.

He laughs hard and we have the best thirty-minute ride I have ever had. He drives fast while telling me about every single building that passes the window.

'This was built by Mussolini. This part is over two thousand six hundred years old. Roma is full of history, Vitoria!'

His English is brilliant: he even says, 'Frankly speaking' and shares his love of British culture. He has two grown-up sons living in London who he visits every year.

'I even know the Queen's theme song, Vitoria!'

'"We Will Rock You"?'

'No!' He laughs and launches into England's national anthem.

I want Fernando to stay with me for the whole week; I am disappointed when we get to the hotel and I have to say goodbye.

'Thank you for such a wonderful welcome to Rome.'

'*Prego*, Vitoria, *prego*.'

I push through a revolving door and find myself in an opulent hall with two huge chandeliers hanging from a domed ceiling. Heavy red drapes surround massive bay windows and paintings with gold frames adorn the walls.

'*Buongiorno.* Checking in?'

'Yes, *bonjourno.*' My plan to stick an 'O' on every French and English word I know is a go.

'Solo?'

'Yes. Solo.'

'No husband today?'

'Not *todayo.*'

'You stay in Rome, alone?'

'Yes ... I ...'

I almost blurt out, 'I – I – I'm running away from my responsibilities for a week because some days I struggle to be the mum I want to be. I'm here to work on my faults, my expectations as a parent and my mindset. This trip will help me re-evaluate my life and make me more grateful for my children all while learning to love myself.'

But I didn't. I say, '*Yeso*, I'm going to the Colosseum tomorrow.'

'Bravo.'

A porter takes my bag and we head up to my room in a wooden lift with rattling doors. Once in my room, I hang up some clothes and open the window. I hear cicadas in the trees, traffic, a police car in the distance, and then music drifting up from a restaurant below.

Rome, alone. Magical. What seemed overwhelming a few hours before now feels like the best choice I have ever made. Time to discover what this city has to teach me.

*

Rome is like an open-air museum. Every turn I take down cobblestoned streets leads me to ancient stone columns jutting from the ground, red-brick ruins, catacombs, beautiful churches with doors as tall as houses and painted ceilings flecked with gold. I walk to the Colosseum and find a café where I sit and stare at this incredible structure that once welcomed 75,000 people at a time to watch gladiators fight to a bloodied and barbaric death. The little brochure I pick up tells me about Roman torture, with pencil drawings of people being drowned, flogged and crucified.

Being so entrenched in history nudges my thoughts. Here I am in a location where people battled for their lives. Where wars were fought and civilisations created, where slaves were tortured, and children ripped from their mother's arms ... yet I can't handle tiffs over who finished my bottle of forest pine bubble bath or who gets to sit in the front seat on the way to school.

Pathetic really.

That afternoon, I walk. I soak up Rome. I drink cold, fresh juice bought from a street vendor, eat bruschetta with tomatoes so sweet they taste like honey, stumble across hidden gardens with palm trees swaying above, surrounded by buildings with stone arches and decorative marble water fountains. The summer sun blazes and I find shade on the steps next to a market stall selling hats, *I love Roma* T-shirts and fridge magnets of the Vatican City. There are people everywhere, tourists leaning in with smiles, tour guides with microphones holding flags on sticks and locals who cut through the crowds with ease. Many smoke as they walk, and I duck under white plumes as I stroll behind.

At night, I eat pizza, sip on lemon sodas and listen to people talking on the tables around me. The Italians are beautiful. A man next to me in tight jeans and crisp shirt holds hands across the table with a dark-haired woman in a floaty silk dress. They share tiramisu from a glass and sip big glasses of vino.

It is weird experiencing it all without anyone to talk to. It doesn't seem right. The time difference means I can't even call. It makes me yearn for their chaos.

After five days of walking the streets of Rome, my friend, Bogfish, arrives from the UK. In our little WhatsApp holiday chat she had said, 'I will come, but I'm skint, let's do it old school.' We decide to act like twenty-year-old interrailers. Backpacks, travel towels and fifty-quid-a-night accommodation.

We spend the next few days snaking along roads that hang from the cliffs around Positano. The steep mountains are sprinkled with villages, and white bell towers jut out from the lush green landscape. Fruit orchards with lemons stand in silent rows on terraces, like giant steps leading up to the sky. In the mornings, we eat custard-filled croissants, drink strong coffees and, when the heat makes us tired, we wander down shaded lanes that lead to crumbling basilicas and up ancient marble steps that open up on to a bustling piazza. It is a holiday spent putting on a few kilos and then trying to walk them off.

I send a few texts to John and the kids, but I don't contact them as much as I should. I need a little bit of space from them, to make some space for me. When we do speak, the internet connection is rubbish and we only manage a few 'I love you's before the screen freezes on four grinning faces.

One day, Bogfish and I get up at dawn to trek along the Path of the Gods, an ancient trail used for hundreds of years to walk between the towns of the Amalfi Coast. As we stride past olive groves and stone walls, in between selfies and rest stops, I tell my friend about my life in Australia.

'Sometimes I shout at my kids, I feel guilty a lot, and have moments of hating being a mum. I am trying to do better but some days I feel like a failure,' I admit.

We chat about how work sneaks past dinnertime and into family time and I feel a lump in my throat when I mention my little Fred, and how I worry for him.

'Parenting makes me scared, and being scared all the time means I get angry or I want to run away.' As I say it, I understand why I really booked this trip.

It isn't to escape them. It is to escape myself.

My kids are just doing what all kids do. Experiencing the full range of emotions, asking questions and working life out day by day. Their little spongy brains are trying to absorb as much as possible, trying to navigate the ups and downs, one blue-iced slushy at a time. It is me who is deciding to react with anger. It's my choice to release the inner troll when something doesn't quite go as I expect. I thought this trip was about needing a break from their issues when – even though it's hard to admit it and I have to swallow a bit of sick as I write it – the only person with an issue is … me.

'Parenting is a huge deal,' says Bogfish. 'You get thrown in and are expected to automatically know what to do. It takes time to become the mum you want to be. We all do things as parents that we look back on and wish we had done differently, Vic, but from what you've said, you see your faults and you're doing everything you can to change them. Being a mum is all about being a work-in-progress. You're doing great.'

(Did I mention that Bogfish is a psychotherapist? I recommend choosing your travel buddies based on skill set.)

I walk behind my friend, with sweat dripping down my temples, feeling a little lighter on my feet. She is right. I am a work-in-progress. A mum who is trying to do better. I can't promise more than that.

When we reach the hilltop looking over Positano, I sit down on a rock. The view is breathtaking.

Yachts glide towards the port, roads twist through tiers of old buildings. I can just make out the rows of white parasols and people dotted along the shore. And even though I am a world away from my family, I have never felt closer.

That night, after our big walk and talk, we check into our next cheap hotel where a lovely young woman called Concetta takes our passports and shows us to our room. There is more than the smell of rotting fruit to greet us – a huge buzzing hornet is ricocheting off the walls. It has a rather pointy sting hanging from its bottom. My own sphincter tightens at the sight of it. I hand Bogfish an espadrille and hide in the cupboard. After some banging, cries of 'come on, you little fucker', I hear the buzz fade.

'It's gone out the window!'

I come out to find shoe prints all over the walls and curtains pulled down from the rails. We tidy up and take a moment to look around the little apartment. There is no aircon or fan and it is thirty-seven degrees at night. The pillows are as flat as sheets of A4 paper and the bed, which has a weird brown stain in the middle, is as hard as a concrete block. My friend and I enter into a tumultuous night, tossing, turning and sweating like a pair of boil-in-the-bag dinners.

The next morning, after unfolding our stiff deckchair bodies into an upright position, there is only one option – ditch the budget accommodation. We pack our bags and get out the credit cards. We spend the last night of our great escape in a posh hotel with soft sheets and a hot tub with a view.

I chink my glass of fizzy water with my friend's and we watch the sun go down over the deep blue Mediterranean Sea.

Even though it is beautiful, I am ready to go home.

Swear Day

I walk through the sliding doors at Brisbane Airport and there they are, holding a piece of paper each, spelling out 'M-U-M-X'. Four smiling faces hide behind the sheets, while a tired nanny stands next to them.

'I'm home. How did it go?' I ask, sort of hoping it has all fallen apart without me.

'Great! It doesn't seem like you've been gone that long,' my husband says in a slightly smug manner.

'Well, I feel like I've been gone forever. Now, group hug.'

I kneel and everyone jumps on me and I know straight away I did the right thing.

We find the car and on the ride home I tell them all about my adventure.

'… and I went to the Sistine Chapel, ate pizza every night, and I watched an opera in Rome by candlelight …'

'Mum, while you were gone, Dad wrote out the house rules and stuck 'em on the fridge for you,' George says. 'They are the same as always, but with a new one. We'll read them out when we get home.'

I've only been away ten days and there's been a regulation enhancement.

When we get home George pulls me over to the fridge and says, 'Right, are you ready? The seven main rules in our house are ...'

1. You are allowed to drink juice straight from the carton/bottle in the fridge.
2. You are never allowed to say no to cuddles.
3. The game Marco Polo must not be played in the pool.
4. Bedrooms to be cleaned up on Wednesdays after school.
5. One new pool inflatable each per year.
6. Korean barbecue only on Sundays.
7. All children are allowed to swear as much as they like one day per year.

'And this is the one we added ...'

8. Mummy is never allowed to go away without us ever again.

'Ahhhhhh that's so sweet. Okay, I promise,' I say, crossing my fingers behind my back. 'One question. When the flipping-nora is Swear Day this year anyway?'

*

Number 7, the swearing rule, I realise is quite controversial. But it, along with camping within a five-kilometre radius, actually the best parenting hack of all time. It took some failing, and letters home from school, to come up with it.

Before the swear rule, Fred was the only preschooler in the world with a swear jar and Nell got in trouble for saying to a support teacher at school that the water balloon 'looks like a big shiny ballbag'. I had to act, before one of them got suspended. So, I created a swear night a few years ago.

'What do you think John?' I ask my husband, 'We let them all swear once a year?'

'I think it's fucking genius,' he chortles. 'Let's do it!' Together we decide which words we will allow. We decide on no c's for anyone and only f's for George.

We choose a night the following week and when it comes round, we stay home, away from police officers, council representatives or members of the local church.

'Right, George,' I say. 'It's Swear Night. The one time a year you are allowed to swear.'

'What? Are you for real?'

'I am for real. Are you excited?'

'Yes, I bloody well am!' he says with a big smile. 'I am going to have the best fucking … wait, can I say fucking?'

'Yes. Fuck away.'

213

'... the best fucking night ever. I'm going to have a few shitting cans of Coke too. This night is going to be the dog's bollocks!'

A pang of regret hits the back of my throat as my angelic boy sprays profanity in every direction. But over the last few cringy years of allowing this fuck-ridden ruling, I have found that my offspring so look forward to this night that they don't swear for the rest of the year. It's like they get it all out in one hit. It rains 'shit', 'piss' and 'wanker's for one magical day and then the clouds part and we are back to 'bother', 'frick' and 'holy fartmuppets!'.

*

I unpack my suitcase onto the bed then I lift out my souvenirs. I untie the string and unfurl cardboard packaging from the ceramic olive oil and balsamic vinegar bottles I bought in Positano. I pop them on my shelf where I can see them and admire the blue painted outlines in the shape of Amalfi villas tucked into the vertical hillside.

I head to the bathroom and sink into a hot bath. I close my eyes and drown out the sound of the argument about Toblerone happening in the lounge and, just for a moment, with my ears under the waterline, I go straight back there.

Bellissima.

Stage Fright

The holiday did what it was meant to and, for once, I'm winning.

Nell got a certificate for being a 'learning legend', Fred wiped his own bum, and my friend Emily texted me to say: *I've just witnessed your proudest moment.*

She had watched on from her car as George was called 'gay' by a renowned mullety bully for having a pink water bottle. George and his best mate, Macen, then held hands and Macen said, 'So what? We're going out to dinner tonight. We've made a reservation!' before they both rolled around on the ground laughing. The bully had apparently blushed, turned around and walked away.

OMG I texted back. *They're my heroes!*

There have also been thank-yous, love-yous, the TV was turned off without me sticking forks in my eyeballs, and not as many kisses have been wiped away.

215

All of this means I'm feeling confident and pleased with myself. The trip has refreshed my outlook on parenting and everyone's swimming along like happy fishes. They're a bunch of learning-legend, bum-wiping, bully-battling heroes! Hurrah!

So, I do what I always do when things go well. I make the stupid decision for us to eat out as a family, in public.

I have blocked our last dinner outing from my memory. (Better it stays locked away, along with childbirth and my first acid trip.) I train myself to forget. It's the only way I keep hold of hope.

My only takeaway from that night was sitting in the car afterwards, crying in my sticky Coca-Cola thongs, surrendering to the realisation we had not yet reached 'The Stage'. It had, yet again, melted through my fingers like glitter slime.

*

'The Stage' is the invisible line in parenting I have watched others get to before me. I've spent years sitting in restaurants wondering why my children were crawling under the table, knocking over drinks and stabbing each other with butter knives, while other families sat straight-backed at the table, making polite comments about the interior design. Their kids are not much older than mine, so I know 'The Stage' is near.

I give it another attempt, and then another. I keep giving my kids the opportunity to prove to me they can do it. That as a family we can order and eat without humiliating ourselves or breaking something. I want to know what it's like to go out and *actually* enjoy myself. When it does happen, I will stand at the school gates and tell every single person who walks past me, 'We did it! You can invite us over to your house now, without risk of your carpets getting ruined or family heirlooms being thrown in the pond. We've reached "The Stage"!'

'I've booked the table for five-thirty,' I tell John.

'Do you remember what happened last time?' my husband replies as he drops his car keys in the pot. 'Don't you ever learn?'

But learning is giving up. I must live in optimism otherwise I will stick my head in the air fryer. Instead of remembering the sad, disgruntled faces of various waitstaff across south-east Queensland, I fantasise.

As I get ready, I imagine how the meal is going to go. I top up my mascara and play out the evening in my mind …

It starts with them all putting on their little outfits (in their rooms by themselves) and each of them coming out, striding down the hall like it's a Paris runway and declaring: 'Right, Mum, I have put my shoes and socks on and I'm ready to go.'

For the boys I imagine smart shirts with bow ties, trousers with braces and flat caps for the boys, like hipster farmers crossed with the Peaky Blinders crime gang. For Nell, a pink dress, a flowery headband, a unicorn-shaped handbag, finished off with Doc Martens. A perfect punk princess.

We all get in the car, seatbelts on and we're off. No traffic. No moaning.

'Gosh Mummy, I am so excited to be going out to dinner tonight. It's so lovely that you and Daddy work so hard to earn money so we can do all these special outings together.' (Too much?)

I imagine arriving at the restaurant and being ushered towards a big mahogany table. Everyone is nodding and smiling as the steaming dishes are placed in front of us. The kids fold napkins into their collars and lick their lips before tucking in. 'What wonderful children you have, so well behaved, and what good eaters!' the waiter says as the kids dab the corners of their mouths with their napkins and place their cutlery together on empty plates.

This fantasy swirls around in my head as I slip on some sandals.

'Kids, go and get ready. We're going out for dinner!'

My words snap me back to reality.

Nell walks out of her bedroom first. I almost ask her for a light. Her hair is piled up on her head like a sumo wrestler with a few scraggly bits hanging down. Electric-blue eye shadow is pasted on her eyelids as thick as peanut butter.

There's red lipstick smeared around her mouth. Her shorts are so tiny I think she borrowed them from her L.O.L. doll. She's wearing stripy socks up to her knees and tiny red sparkly shoes like Dorothy's from *The Wizard of Oz*.

'I hope there's a good podiatrist in Kansas.'

'What?'

'Nothing darling, you look lovely,' I lie.

She reminds me of a lady I saw in a US crime documentary who ran a crack den in downtown Detroit.

'There is just one thing. Could you take a bit of make-up off, please? I can't see your pretty face.'

'No. I like it like this.'

George appears in a Hawaiian shirt with the buttons done up wrong. His hair is slicked back like Al Pacino in *The Godfather* and he's wearing trainers that look like clown shoes. I almost expect him to put on a rainbow wig, do a forward roll, and honk a horn.

'Your trainers look a bit too big. Are they the ones Max gave you? You might want to save them for a few years ... when they fit.'

'They're fine,' he grumbles. 'Can I play Roblox for five minutes until we leave?'

'Okay. Honk, honk,' I say and squeeze the air.

He doesn't blink. He just internally confirms that yes, his mother is mad, turns and walks back down the hallway, tripping over his shoes as he goes.

Then Fred, with swimming shorts on backwards, a pyjama top and thongs on the wrong feet.

Deep breath.

In through the nose out through the mouth. *Farrrrrrrrrrrrk.* I'm glad *I* don't have to save my swearing for one night per year.

Our local RSL club is a modern building with high ceilings and a huge glass frontage. When you enter, there are plaques on the wall in memory of unknown soldiers and an old musket with a green army helmet displayed in a tall glass cabinet. We head to the corner for our normal table.

The kids take off their shoes, pop them into the rack and head into the play area where there's a slide and some computer games. We order the same every time. One fish and chips, one pizza and a children's steak. The salmon for Mum. The burger for Dad. All with a free ice cream.

Then the lights dim.

In RSLs all over the country at six o'clock each night, they play the 'Last Post'. A dedication to soldiers lost in all the wars. In our RSL, trumpets sound out and a video is played. This two-minute interlude is the only time my children ever behave perfectly. Even if they're in the middle of a game of Bullrush, they stand up, put their hands down by their sides, and hold their chins high like footguards at Buckingham Palace. The sight of them, through the glass window in the play area, standing as still as statues fills my heart.

It's downhill from there.

A lost Fred (found sitting in the gambling room). A fall off the slide (red mark, no swelling). A broken PS4 controller (that we offer to pay for). Three drinks tipped over (Fanta on my white dress). A poo as dinner arrives (sixteen minutes). A piece of steak regurgitated onto a plate (medium-rare). An argument over who has the biggest chip (me). A banged head on the corner of the table (ice). A lost teddy (found stuffed in the shoe rack). A shouting match about leaving the play area to eat. (NOW!)

I sit, sipping on a fizzy water when I can. I look around. There is food on the floor, but most is still on abandoned plates. My children are fickle foodies.

'Kids, can you all come back here and finish your dinner? You've hardly eaten anything. You love pizza. It's your favourite.'

'I don't like it today.'

'So, why did you order it then?'

'I like pizza, not this pizza. The cheese is funny.'

'You can't have your ice cream unless you eat all your dinner.'

I stick to my threat.

Once the kids have nibbled on a few more chips, and some pizza crust, they all go back to the play area. My husband and I sit for a moment. We say nothing. My vacation glow has well and truly faded away. We are both tired and fed up with our own voices repeating the same demands, and 'The Stage' still feels very out of reach.

'Is this normal?' I ask him. 'Are we asking too much of them? I mean, is it really that hard to sit still and eat food without us micromanaging their every move? I know we're handling it a bit better than before, but still, I'm bloody over it! How long does this level of parenting go on for?'

'They're just kids. We'll get there.'

'Will we? Everything feels so hard sometimes.'

I'm going to end this meal like I did the last one. As my eyes fill with tears, my husband takes my hand and says in a very sage voice, 'It's not always going to be perfect.'

I use a few napkins to clear up the spillages and give the kids a five-minute warning. My husband is right. Not being perfect is okay. It's a lesson I need reminding of often. I forget my kids are allowed to make mistakes, break stuff, not listen and regurgitate steaks onto plates. It's what kids do. I'm the one with the fantasy, not them. I'm the one putting pressure on them to grow up and act like hoity-toity twits in a restaurant. It's me, desperate for them to grow up before they are ready. It's me, searching for who I was before I became a mum. Searching for a break in the chaos. It's me, having unfair expectations. It's me not allowing my kids time.

I need to slow down.

'We are not at "The Stage" yet and that's okay,' I say to John when we get in the car. 'I think we need to wait before we go out again. It makes me feel angry and it's not their fault. Let's just stay home for a few more years.'

'Good idea.'

On the way home I play some loud drum-and-bass, and we all jiggle up and down like bouncy balls when the bassline drops. I feel mean about the ice cream ban, so I pull in at Coles and grab some donuts. We all sit in the carpark, sugar on our faces, sticky fingers, talking with our mouths full and with jam squirting out onto our clothes. The Stage is here. It's now. I just hadn't seen it before.

Zombies in the Garden

October

Over the following weeks, I don't force my children to go out to dinner. There are no expectations or weird bow ties in sight. Instead, we have dippy dinners at home: cheese boards, grapes, chips and dips with thick slices of sourdough. I also buy a Kmart plug-in hotplate along with five pairs of tongs and we make a mess cooking meat and veggies on the hotplate. The kids love it and I get to relax a little bit. Apart from the odd 'hot fat in the eye' incident, it's a hit. No angry waitstaff or piles of wet paper napkins in sight.

I feel pretty smug about transforming a habit. I'm accepting where we're at as a family and letting the kids just 'be' a bit more. Having certain expectations of them was making me disappointed. Predicting chaos is somehow more comforting than being surprised by it. I am now hurtling towards the end of the year having made a few clumsy leaps forward.

It's time to start planning for our annual Halloween party. Last year's was a wet lettuce. A massive storm blew the giant inflatable ghost into a tree, the creepy pathway flooded and I was at high risk of electrocution. My outfit included a huge metal magpie duct-taped to my shoulder, which acted like a lightning rod. No one showed up, no tricks and no treats, just pumpkin-shaped soggy sandwiches on the deck. But the kids love Halloween so, instead of backing out, I decide to take it up a notch and give my little monsters a Halloween to remember.

It's time to do the one thing I have *always* wanted to do. The 'Thriller' dance.

I call up some other local mums and tell them the plan.

'We'll make outfits and at the party we'll perform it as a surprise for the kids. It will be the best day of our lives!'

I must have been very convincing because by bedtime I have eight mums signed up. I book our local community centre one evening a week for seven weeks of rehearsals and lie to the children.

'I'm going to yoga class. See you later.'

Then I sneak off.

The mums meet in the dark entrance way of the local community centre. We are all excited, which causes us to put the wrong number in the security system six times and sets all the alarms off. Once we make it inside, we head to the little room at the back and switch on the lights. The

Kookaburra suite is tiny, just enough space for us all to stand a metre apart. It is all we need. We wheel a TV into the space and stand in two rows like army cadets waiting for a command.

My sister, Louise, who lives nearby, is our dance leader. Our 'Michael'. She has been beavering away at home before the first get-together, learning the moves and counting the steps.

'Right girls, this is it.'

She points a controller at the TV and a YouTube clip begins. The creaky door at the start of the song makes us all turn to one another and smile. The hairs on my arms bristle.

The dance crew on the screen are limber, pink leotard-clad professionals, with soft puffy hair and tight buns. They perform each move, making it look easy, smooth.

'One, two, three and up.'

'Turn, turn, pull and turn.'

We watch it all the way through once, take a deep breath, and get into position.

We copy the dancers, but it doesn't look the same. We look more like Ricky Gervais from *The Office*. I'm glad there are no floor-to-ceiling mirrors in the room otherwise I may have given up.

I trip over my feet, trainers squeak, another mum slips over, there is huffing and some swearing.

'For fuck's sake. I just can't get the pelvic thrusts right. Let's take it from the top.'

For three hours, every Monday, we practise our moves. We strut up and down with our hands like T-rexes, we drop to the floor and rise from the dead, we shuffle, pivot, sidestep, squat and shimmy. We even have a growl moment. It's wonderful.

No matter how hard it is or how silly we look, we never, ever give up.

'Turn, turn, pivot, turn.'

'Monster walk. That's it.'

'We're getting it!!'

'Over the shoulder.'

'Now, one, two, three and howl.'

'Ahhwoooooooooo.'

*

On the morning of our surprise show, the kids are at school and some of the mums come over to help me decorate the house. We pin posters of Frankenstein's monster to the walls, cover tables in spidery tablecloths and make green lemonade with plastic eyeballs floating around in it. Then we get our outfits ready. We tear up bedsheets, rip apart shirts and trousers, backcomb our hair, paint our faces white, draw black rings around our eyes and drip red food colouring on everything. We are sufficiently zombified.

Kids and parents stream in through the front gate carrying plates of spooky food and we mingle in the crowd, just like all the other partygoers there, dressed up as awakened corpses. Nobody knows what will soon be unleashed.

John manages to get all the children to sit in rows in the front garden and Louise hits *play*.

The creaky door.

From different areas of the garden the zombie mums, arms outstretched, one leg dragging, head towards the deck.

Then, we do the best, most brilliant, most spectacular 'Thriller' dance the southern hemisphere has ever witnessed. Every move as tight as the leotard-wearing YouTubers. It's perfect.

As the music ends, we collapse and bite into the blood capsules hidden in our cheeks and as we lay twitching on the ground, blood spills from our mouths … and everyone cheers.

This is it, I think. *I am now the coolest mum in the whole world and I will be forgiven for all my past indiscretions. I am the mum who spent weeks secretly learning the 'Thriller' dance to entertain her children for four minutes twenty seconds. I win.*

Nell (a vampire) and George (a skeleton) walk over to me. I kneel, wipe away tears of joy and spread my arms out wide, expecting them to leap on me and tell me how marvellous it was.

Nell says, 'Can I have a gummy snake now?'

And George says, 'Are we going to do apple-bobbing?'

That is it.

No, *well done*. No *thank you*. Not even a cuddle. It was as if 'the one thing I have always wanted to do' never happened. They dawdle off in the opposite direction looking for another glass of 'Fang' Fanta.

I bow my head. My big parenting leap forward has just moonwalked backwards.

My children's reaction to my 'Thriller' dance is supposed to be the moment our relationship changes forever and we skip off into a graveyard under the light of a full moon, knowing that, no matter what, 'My mum did the "Thriller" dance once and everything will be okay now.'

A feeling of disappointment hangs off me like the little plastic spiders carefully sewn to my torn T-shirt.

I sit down and watch the party carry on. John (a crazy doctor, splattered in blood, wearing a bald cap) gets pelted with giant eyeballs (water balloons). Kids sink hands into buckets of witches' guts to find rubber bat toys (fifteen packets of spaghetti dyed with two bottles of red food colouring) and the parents stand around sipping on flutes of Dracula's piss (alcohol-free wine). Everyone is having the best time, but I feel a bit sad. Like all the effort is never appreciated.

*

My husband finds me sitting in a corner of the party. Just like in the restaurant a few weeks before, he has come over to make me feel better.

'You all right?'

'I'm all right. It's just that I feel like I can't make them happy. I give them the world and they want the universe. Nothing I do is good enough.'

'You're amazing. They will remember that forever. Now, go and put your feet up and have a rest while I get rid of everyone and tidy up.'

I do as the spooky doctor says. I sneak off to my bedroom and lie on the bed. I close my eyes and try to mentally fight off never feeling like enough. I push my negative thoughts aside and desperately try to think about how grateful I am for the great ungrateful …

They're just kids, I say to myself. *They'll appreciate me one day.*

I hear people laughing, the front gate opening and closing, plates being stacked in the dishwasher and, as the house quietens, I drift off to sleep.

*

'Mum!'

Someone is calling me. It's dark outside. I must have been asleep for hours.

'Mum! Come down to the lounge!'

Just in case they've set light to the couch, I get up, put my dressing gown on and head towards the direction of their calls.

When I get there, they are all standing in a row facing the TV. The screen is black and all I can see reflected in it are three smiling faces.

'Press *play*,' George whispers as he nudges his sister.

Then, I hear a creaky door.

I'm Actually Allergic
to Cleaning

Nell is in her bedroom. The clock is ticking.

A minute for each year of their lives is what I learnt at the Sunny Days Parenting course.

If the 3-2-1 method doesn't work, then another option is a timeout.

I sit on the couch, wishing Nell was much older than eight.

'Can I come out now?'

'No, three more minutes of calm down-time.'

All I asked her was to do a quick tidy-up of her room.

She refused. Just as she threw a pair of knickers at my head, I have a flashback.

Me, at seven years old, sitting on my patchwork quilt, with my mum standing over me.

'Victoria, this room is disgusting.'

She got down on her hands and knees and started pulling items from the dark gap under the bed.

'Shoving everything under your bed is not cleaning up. Look, there are dirty plates and cups under here. And what's this?'

She was holding an antique porcelain doll wearing a creepy Edwardian lace dress. One of its arms was missing and what looked like horsehair was sprouting from its insides.

'I gave you this because I thought you'd like to play with it, not so you could break it. You never look after people's things. You're staying up here until this room is tidy.'

I used to loathe cleaning my bedroom. Just the thought of it made my body tired and heavy, the same feeling I get when visiting a museum. I used to try and get away with a half-arsed, forearm sweep of everything left out on the countertops into the top drawers. I could not keep my room tidy. Cleaning wasn't in my make-up. Still isn't.

My kids are the same. They don't notice the mess, they just walk through it, step over it, and add to it. I feel like a backwards Hansel and Gretel, picking up a trail of breadcrumbs rather than leaving them behind. Some days, I conduct tests. I will find a mouldy tangerine and place it strategically near the front door or in the centre of the bathroom, just to see if anyone else bothers to deal with it. I make a note in my diary, *Tangerine Ground Zero*, and diarise its lifespan.

Day One: Unmoved. Starting to smell.
Day Four: Unmoved. Skin going hairy.

Day Eight: Kicked. New HQ near coffee table. Pungent.
Day Fourteen: Dog licked it.
Day Sixteen: Task Force Tangerine has surrendered.

There could be a rotting corpse lying on the kitchen bench and the kids would dump their school bags on it and ask what's for dinner.

I am also not very keen on hanging up clothes. My husband likes to say I suffer from piles, because a stream of dirty clothes seems to spew from my behind. I abhor bleaching toilets, dusting or ironing. The only time I've ever touched an iron was at university when I was eighteen. I pressed damp cigarette rolling papers that were screwed up in the back pocket of my jeans. I was carefully preparing them for the *Withnail and I*–style 'Camberwell carrot' joint I planned on assembling that morning.

I know this may sound like a lie, but actually, I am allergic to cleaning. I have a dust allergy, which means I have to put on four tops each morning before I find one that doesn't make me sneeze. If I *am* going to clean, I prep by taking an antihistamine and sticking pieces of bog roll up each nostril. It's not a great look to have when the man who comes to read the electricity meter stops by. I wish I was allergic to the children too, but I am not sure that telling my husband that they make my throat itchy and I can't be in the same room as them would go down too well.

I really don't know how other mums do it. My friends' houses are all pristine. Clean lines and shiny surfaces. Maybe they all did an online course in cushion plumping. Their floors are mopped, blinds are dusted and their clothes don't smell of stale sick.

The difference is … that they do chores and I don't.

So, the chores pile up, one boring job on top of another. Instead of tackling them, I distract myself with minor thrill-seeking activities. I drive around carparks the wrong way, have races at traffic lights, steal grapes at the supermarket. I sit and play the kids' computer games when they're at school. I'm a *Zelda* champion. I eat hidden packets of Sour Patch Kids and toss toys in their rooms just hard enough for them not to break, but hard enough for me to relieve some aggression. Sometimes I listen to the Wiggles at full volume in the car when there are no children. I sing 'Rock-A-Bye Your Bear' at traffic lights and get concerned looks from strangers.

I also go to the Plaza to use the toilet and keep the door open. I sit there, in peace, staring at the sinks and line of mirrors, feeling rebellious. If I hear someone come in, I slam the cubicle door closed with my foot.

Nothing to see here, love!

While I am off gallivanting, escaping cleaning duties, there is only one other person available to pick up the slack. My husband, Poor John.

Unfortunately for Poor John, I don't adhere to old-school procedures made up by men with inferiority complexes and small penises back in 1880. I'm not 'a homemaker'. I'm a bad wife. A naughty wife. I'm the sort of wife who doesn't put lids on things properly. I'm the one who balances a fresh roll of toilet paper on top of the empty tube and ignores the rotten cucumber in the bottom of the fridge.

On Sundays, Poor John does 'the pile'.

Doing 'the pile' propels my poor husband into god-like status where I live. Women are, in equal measure, sympathetic towards him for marrying so unwisely and in awe of him for taking on this archaic female role.

The term 'Poor John' has become a bit of a saying.

'Poor John. He's got so much on. He's so busy yet always has time for the kids and the washing pile. He's such a great dad. He must be exhausted.'

'What do you mean, "Poor John"?' I grumble.

'You know, him having to do the washing and everything.'

Yes, my poor husband, I think, *stuck in an equal marriage with a woman who knows her worth. It's just awful.*

I wait for my friend to tell me how brilliant I am, or at least a, 'He couldn't do it without you.'

It doesn't come.

'Oh, Poor John. He's a keeper, Vic.'

I want to punch her in the face.

It's not just the washing he gets praised for. If he drops the kids at school, people probably stare in wonderment. 'Oh, what a great dad. So involved.' If he takes them to the café, women fawn over him. 'Wow, he really is a devoted father.' When he carried our babies in a sling, people stopped in the street. 'Look, there he is, the king of men, carrying his offspring. Poor guy, his wife must be dead.'

My 'poor' husband puffs out his chest like a pigeon and looks around to see if anyone else has noticed how amazing he is. He fancies himself with a baby carrier on and, when Nell paints his toenails, he leaves the polish on for months as if it's a bloody parenting medal of honour.

When my husband hoovers, he doesn't just hoover. He takes the cushions off the couch and cleans underneath. He stands on chairs sucking up cobwebs, then rams the swivel brush on the end and goes into places no one sees or has ever been, behind the fridge and under the oven. He hoovers books, teddies, computer keyboards and plants. He hoovers like his life depends on it. His style of hoovering is designed to put mine to shame. He hoovers once a year. He doesn't say anything as he does it, just whistles in a very irritating way. But I know what he's thinking – *I will show her what hovering really looks like* – as he shoves the never-used-before nozzle behind the microwave.

There are a few tasks that are distributed more fairly.

I organise every aspect of our social lives, he mows the lawn.

I choose what to watch on Netflix, he agrees.

He does all the accounts, I hide Kmart receipts.

And somehow, it works.

But alas, today I am on my own. Poor John is at work and I have to use my teeny-weeny lady brain to work this one out.

Nell is still in her room.

'I'm sorry, Nell. We have done the countdown, an eight-minute timeout and now, I'm afraid to say, because your room is still a mess I am going to have to cancel your playdate with Mim.' I say it calmly. She bursts into tears.

I know making my child cry sounds like a fail, but a year ago I would have been shouting so loudly that I would have had to knock on my neighbour's door to say, 'No, there has not been a stabbing. Just another messy bedroom. Sorry for the racket. No need to be alarmed.'

Today, I kneel in front of Nell and go to put my arms around her. I've done well. Handled the situation like a proper parent.

Nell looks up and, with a face like hellfire, grabs my forearms and digs her nails in as hard as she can.

'I hate you!'

I don't react. I just get up and walk out of her room.

I go and sit on the end of my bed.

What's the point? I think. *What is the point of even trying?*

No one cares, no one can hear me. I am an inconsequential blob. My rules or attempts at being better mean nothing. What is the point in me trying to parent, when all I get in return is this.

I look at my arms. The curve of her nails. This is what makes mumming hard.

The steps back.

*

After some long chats about 'hurting people not being okay', I drop Nell to school a bit late. Then I do the shop, leave my wallet in Coles, drop a bottle of milk, stub my toe and, after a conciliatory almond croissant, get a tummy ache.

It's only 1.30 pm and I feel like going to bed. I decide not to go home because the house is a mess, so I sit in the school carpark for an hour, crying. I place my forehead on the steering wheel and just let it all out. I sound like a humpback whale in mating season. In between bouts of sniffling and moaning, I check that the windows of the car are closed so no one can hear the yowl of a broken parent.

There's a knock on my window. It's a mate of mine. One of the shiny diamonds. I push the button and the window rolls down. She passes me a brown paper bag, says nothing, reaches out, squeezes my shoulder blade and leaves.

I open the bag and inside there is a bar of chocolate and a piece of paper. I unfold it and read:

Sometimes parenting is fucked.

There it is. The truth. In four magical words. She hasn't stopped to offer me advice, say 'you should do this' or 'why don't you try this'. She doesn't even ask me how I am feeling because she already knows. There is no judgement, no asking why I am crying in the school carpark.

My friend's note not only takes some weight and guilt off my shoulders, it also reminds me there are lots of mums crying in school carparks all over the world, mums who are always doing their best and not always getting it right.

I eat the chocolate, fold the note and put it in my wallet so I can read it whenever I have a bad day. The bell goes, I take a deep breath ... and mum.

'Hey Nellie, how was your day?'

'It was okay.'

'What would you like for dinn—' Before I can finish my question Nell has tugged my top and I stop on the path. When I look down, she has tears shining in her eyes and her lip is trembling.

'I'm sorry I hurt you this morning. I didn't mean to. I love you, Mummy. I won't do it again.'

I crouch and give her a cuddle. 'It's okay, Nell. I love you too.'

One step back, two forward.

Some Drivel About
Moving Forward

The last few months have been healing, and if I do still lose the plot occasionally I am not being so hard on myself. Some days are just fucked and that's okay. Instead of shouting, I look for practical solutions. This week I have not bought any coffees from the local café and instead I have put the money in a jar to go towards a cleaner. A proper one, who I'm not married to.

Before she shows up, the kids and I clean faster and harder than we have ever done in our entire lives.

'C'mon, you lot. The cleaner's coming today!'

Never before have my children acted more hastily to a command. 'The cleaner's coming' is the equivalent of 'The Man' or having a red-hot poker up the bottom. George rushes past in a swathe of bed sheets. Nell sweeps up beads from under her bed and Fred … well, I'm not sure what he is doing. He is sitting on the wooden floor, naked, next to a bowl of hot water, a tea towel, a spoon and a packet of elastic bands. I let him do his thing and I empty the bins.

The dog barks as she arrives with mops and buckets. She looks annoyed. She takes out an extendable duster and then huffs and puffs her way around the house. Her mood is resentful. It seems all people, even if it's their job, hate cleaning. I get it.

The house is gleaming once she's finished. The dried oatmeal has been chipped off the inside of the microwave, the hairy soap is as good as new and she's even managed to get the soy sauce stains out of the bottom off the condiment cabinet. But, even though we've all put in the effort for the cleaner, our house is still overflowing.

We live in a bungalow with no storage. It's one of those old Queenslanders that never looks completely spotless. Brightly coloured plastic toys spill out of cupboards, spare quilts bulge out of big storage bags, baskets of teddies are shoved under beds, and the clothes, my god, the clothes, are stuffed into every cavity. Sorting it all out is not a job for the cleaner.

Which means the time has come for the transformative … life-changing … sneeze-inducing … mega clean.

I start by putting the kettle on, sitting down and having a nice cuppa. I watch a program on Netflix about minimising household junk. Marie Kondo rolls up T-shirts and makes homeowners part with boxes of CDs. There are guidelines:

purposeful possessions only, one is enough, a place for everything, simple is best, and quality over quantity. It looks liberating. I finish my tea, have a small nana nap and about two hours later decide I had better do something useful. I put on some trackies, a mask, tie my hair up in a bun, take an antihistamine and get stuck in. My plan is to clear some space ... so that I can fill it up again.

I fill a trailer with all sorts of weird items that have made a comfy home in my cupboards. A popcorn machine, two broken fans, some cookery books, shot glasses, a chemistry set, a tonne of baby clothes, a dog flap, about ten unused scented candles, a solo gumboot, pillows that have those frightening yellow stains on them, a broken umbrella, out-of-date pasta and a whole basket of craft materials. I sift through some bills, boxes and papers in the office, and come across drawings and paintings the kids have done. I don't throw them into the 'special box' (the bin) or douse them all in petrol and set them on fire, I collect them. I make a little pile.

In a rare moment of niceness, I decide to put the precious 'artworks' into scrapbooks. It's a very out-of-character mumsy move. I create a workspace, put glue, scissors and cello tape out on the dining room table and spend a whole afternoon making each of my children a big memory book.

Inside, I stick letters from Santa, correspondence with the Tooth Fairy (one that says: *Dear Tooth Fairy, You know the drill. Love George*), locks of hair, school certificates, tracings of small hands, flattened-out Easter bonnets, birthday cards, cinema tickets, photos and the little plastic hospital bracelets given to each of them on the day they were born.

I sprinkle glitter and add a few *You've got this* and *Wow!* stickers for decorations and feel extremely smug by the time they get home.

'Look, I've made each of you a memory book. You can add to it if there is anything you want to keep.'

They spend an hour, kneeling together on the floor, going through them, and shouting out.

'I didn't know you kept this!' George says as he holds up a swimming certificate.

'I 'member this, Mummy. My owl painting,' says Fred.

'Mum, why is there a tooth in here when the fairy should have taken it?' Nell doesn't miss a trick.

'That's a dog tooth. They get sent back.'

'Oh, okay.'

'I can't believe you kept my umbilical cord, Mum!' George is now holding up an envelope that contains a bit of dried flesh.

'Well, it didn't seem right to throw it away!'

The books are a hit. It's gone so well I feel like continuing the niceties, so we go to the rolled ice cream parlour.

They get three large cookies and cream with marshmallows. They watch the man expertly scrape the ice-cream mixture off the big icy plate. He picks up each curl with tongs and places it in a cup.

As soon as the sugar hits the bloodstream, moods start to undo at the seams.

'You've got more than me.'

'Nell said she hates me.'

'Right, stop that, we've had a lovely day, let's not ruin it.' I manhandle the kids into a row on a bench and pull out my phone for a photo. 'Smile and pretend you like each other for a moment.'

They shuffle in close, holding their ice-cream cups. I get two cheesy grins and one death stare. Two out of three is not bad.

I post the photo on Instagram, a happy shot that makes my life look #blessed. Instagram is where I share the highlights, the smiles, the constant happiness. I make myself look like the mum who has it all.

I hate posting, it makes me anxious, but I can't stop. I have a schedule with socials, like it's a job I don't get paid for. My posts go like this:

I do a Nature post. (A close-up of a raindrop on a leaf.)

Then an Exercise post. (A walk with happy, waggy dog.)

A Family post. (Look how crazy and lovable my kids are!)

A Sober Me post. (Drinking tea and looking content.)

An Inspirational Quote post. (Some drivel about moving forward.)

Then, back to the Nature post. (A fucking colourful flower or something.)

Online humblebrags give the impression that my life is perfect. A great mum who has achieved balance and contentment. This online still life is half true. I *am* like that sometimes. I have moments of amazing parenting. It's not all 'stop it's, 'drop it's, and 'timeout's. There are breaks in the rain when life goes well, believe it or not.

I capture the kids' lives, share the special moments, freeze-frame the milestones. Tiny newborns in knitted hats, messy toddlers covered in paint, proud first days at school, buckets and spades on holidays and family shots. All of us huddled together, five heads in a square, beaming. I take pictures to remember our good days, flawless flashes in between everyday clashes.

Those happy times are the memories I want to keep, to hold. They are the scrapbook moments of our lives. The days when the mummy I know is within me shines out.

On days with Fred, if he is poorly or just needs another 'Mummy day', we eat pancakes and watch movies. We read books and sing songs about frogs and get all the teddies out for a picnic in the lounge. He still has a lunchtime nap some days and I hold him as his eyes close, his little body heating mine like a hot water bottle, his thumb dropping from his mouth as he drifts into a deep sleep.

There are days with Nell in which she sighs 'I love you, Mummy' every two minutes. We get the sewing machine out to make a dolly dress, we plug the glue gun in and stick beads to toilet rolls, and at night when she's in the bath, I wash her hair and list all the wonderful things in her life, so she doesn't have bad dreams.

'Think about monkeys riding bikes, Nell. And unicorns dancing. Water slides and mermaids. Eating scrambled eggs and going to get our nails done. Think about holidays and playdates, cuddles with Tigger, and how much Mummy and Daddy love you.'

Then my days with George, my big boy. We go to a concert or a walk up Mount Coolum. Just us against the world. I know he's happy because he skips instead of walking and he talks nonstop, about everything. He jabbers about crushes, a skateboarding move, and *Fortnite*. He asks questions about being a teenager and laughs when I swear, but never swears himself (except one day a year). Sometimes he comes to boxing with me, just to have that car journey without anyone else. He plugs in my iPhone and I teach him about music, everything from gangster rap to Britpop, and we sing 'Wonderwall' at full volume.

His favourite time of the day is when the others are asleep, and he has us all to himself.

'Remember when it was just me, Mum, before the other two came along? Good times.'

We make late-night raisin toast and watch documentaries, snuggled up on the couch with a blanket over us, our toes meeting in the middle, wiggling to get warm.

George still holds my hand when we cross a road … but the before-school cheek pecks are beginning to dwindle.

I know these times are special. The best of my life. The years I will forever long for when they are gone. But instead of sitting back and soaking them up I try to save them, capture these moments, and add them to my Instagram grid. So that I never forget.

*

When I first left home at eighteen, it wasn't because I was ready, it was because I was angry. My last conversation with my parents went something like:

'We will not be spoken to like that, Victoria.'

'I don't care. I hate you. You are both twats.'

'In that case, you should leave.'

'All right, then. I bloody well will.'

I turned my back and as I stepped onto the stone driveway, a tear dripped down my cheek. I hadn't wanted it to end like this, but the large amount of drugs and alcohol pumping around my bloodstream made me a difficult houseguest. I packed a bag, stole fifty quid out of the envelope in Mum's bedside table, grabbed a couple of tins of beans, a sleeping bag, a handful of cassette tapes, and I was off.

I drove a Morris Minor back then and even though my parents had confiscated the keys I managed to wheel-spin out of the drive after starting the engine by twisting the ignition with a two pence piece.

In my rear-view mirror, I saw my mum at the window. Both of us knew this wasn't the way to 'go about things'. But it was too late. The photos on the wall were fading and the good memories too far away to grasp on to.

I managed on my own. I got a job. I made friends. I survived, just. I ate pasta and drank free beer. I got boyfriends who paid for petrol, and I borrowed coins for the laundrette. After six months of not speaking, my mum and dad knocked on the door where I was living.

'I've missed you,' I said before I remembered I was a sulky teen.

'We've missed you too.'

And that was that. We hugged and went for fish and chips on the seafront.

The thought of my children leaving like I did, after an argument, fills me with dread. I can't imagine not speaking to them for a day, let alone six months.

*

'George, what are you going to do when you are eighteen?' I ask one day during a family walk.

'Go and be a dive instructor in Thailand. Don't worry, Mum, you can come too.'

'What about you, Nell?'

'I will marry Daddy and live at home with you, forever.'

'You can't do that!' I laugh, but in my head, I imagine bolting the doors, putting barbed wire along the fence and installing a high-tech security system so they can never leave.

Watching them get older is wonderful in so many ways, but it's also painful. It represents them nearing their departure.

My heart breaks as I write this.

No more warm lunchtime naps, no more dancing unicorns or teddy-bear picnics.

No more sighs of 'I love you, Mummy' and no more wiggly toes. With each passing day, I see his hand slipping from mine; her pursed lips replaced by a cheek when I lean in for a kiss; his back turning as he walks from me; all of them walking away to a life of their own. I can't bear the thought of them being gone; part of my heart will be carved from my chest.

'Blink and you'll miss it,' people say, and it does feel like the sands of their young lives are slipping through the hourglass. So, I keep hoarding the memories. It's how I keep them close. It's how I keep them home.

I open my Instagram account and upload a photo of us all together, smiling next to the lighthouse in Byron Bay. We're wearing different coloured raincoats, hair is windswept, and our cheeks are red from the hike. It's a lovely picture. I write a cheesy blurb underneath it and add #grateful – then delete it, because everybody knows only twats do that – and click the share button.

I plump a cushion, sit back. I take a moment to look around the room. It's nice to see it tidy for once, it even smells clean, like frangipani. The muddy trainers are lined up near the front door, colourful pencils that were spread out on the dining room table now in glass jars, and even the handprints on the glass bifold doors are gone. There are no soggy cornflakes tipped over near the sink, and the school bags are all piled up nicely in a corner. Remnants of my children in every nook and cranny. It's soothing having their belongings around me.

My hope is that this is where we begin. That our home, when messy or tidy, is where the foundations of happy people are laid. By clearing up, putting old memories into scrapbooks and getting rid of clutter filling up our cupboards, I'm making space for the future ... so that photos hanging on the walls won't be reminders of good times gone by. My children will be.

Equally on Different Days

Since creating the scrapbooks, I've made a firm promise to myself to not be on my phone as much. Capturing every single moment of the kids' lives is taking up too much time, and could be considered slightly obsessive. I have a new tactic for the parenting toolbox and it's working: I only use my phone when I am standing up.

As soon as I need to google the population of South-East Asia or search for a fish taco recipe, I stand up and shout, 'Can someone please find my glasses?' They all respond in unison, 'They're on your head, Mum.' I then do what I need to do, and sit back down.

I have halved my time online this week. Actually, I'm standing up now. My mum has sent me a text.

Hellllo Bucky. Dad ... ... at hoshpissshdtn f Needed eyes out. I cannt go there anymore after the rude man Lov Mum. Cccccc

There is a horse head emoji at the end. It's either a threat or a mistake. When I see her later that day, I ask for an explanation, which turns out to be much more entertaining than I expect.

My eighty-one-year-old mother returned to her car that was parked in the hospital's multi-storey carpark. She had been in a hurry to take my dad for an eye operation and the vehicle wasn't exactly parked between the white lines. A note protruded from under her windscreen wiper. She plucked it out, unfolded it, and in thick black marker someone had written: *SHIT PARK, CUNT.*

There was even a comma.

'Was it a shit park?' I ask.

'Well,' she says, 'he got the first bit right. It was a shit park. I was in a hurry to take your dad in, and the car was a bit wonky. But he got the second bit wrong. It happened today, which is a Friday, and I'm only a cunt on Wednesdays!'

I nearly choked on my custard cream.

We have a natter and a giggle about the note and I spend the rest of the afternoon at their house, sitting with my parents. Dad is doing a crossword, occasionally shouting out clues.

'Seven letters, starting in P, something-something-D, where horses graze.'

We both shout back 'Paddock' in unison.

Mum tells me about her book club and a recipe she's going to try for a dinner party this coming weekend.

'I'm going to do individual spicy Moroccan lamb pies with mash and make the sauce from scratch. If it all goes wrong, I've got chicken liver pâté and some blue cheese soup in the freezer. They can have that.'

'Sounds yummy,' I say.

We get on so well some days, feet up, cup in hand, sharing funny anecdotes about our lives. I love being near her. Her filthy humour and freckles bring me comfort. But sometimes we can't be in the same room. Our relationship can change as quickly as a traffic light. I hate it when we are at odds with one another, but we are both too stubborn to apologise, so our fallouts tend to go on longer than they should. It's a relationship stalemate that I'm sure is pretty normal when you love someone that much.

It's the same with the kids. Their emotions are like a bag of liquorice allsorts – I'm never sure what I'm going to get from one day to the next. If one is up, another is down. I usually have one happy kid and two dissatisfied ones. To an outsider it might look like I have a favourite. And honestly, sometimes I do.

Having a golden child runs in my family. My gran had favourites. When my dad was a boy, she said to him, 'You always love your first-born more.' Dad was her second child. I'm not sure how this affected him growing up. He's eighty-five and doesn't seem to have much trauma to deal with. His only traumatic occurrences nowadays are losing to my brother at Wordle and answering a FaceTime call. But he tells the story often, so I am guessing being number two (out of two) had some impact. Also, he doesn't speak to his brother often anymore.

The truth is, I know how my grandmother felt.

My favourite changes depending on the day.

There is an affection hierarchy in my house, and it is based upon hormones, their behaviour and whoever finds the hairbrush. I'm not one of those mums who can say I love them all equally all the time.

Instead, I stagger my love out like a relay race.

I will give you an example of this before you, the reader, report me to the authorities. Don't worry! It levels out like butter eventually, spreading equally, covering all corners.

George became school captain this year, so lately, I have been a bit nicer to him than the others. I take him to the plaza and I laugh at his surreal *knock knock* jokes. (Knock knock. Who's there? A potato. A potato who? I'm a potato with a sausage willy. Erm okay, please don't tell that one at school.) I allow him to watch Instagram reels on my phone more than I should. The other two take second and third place on the love podium until he trips up.

After a few days of being top kid, he gets cocky. My love-bombing has accidentally given him a false sense of security. He watches the iPad without asking, claims ownership of the TV controller and then helps himself to my secret supply of chocolate-covered honeycomb. The final one is a step too far.

So, then it happens … my love transfers.

I lock on to Nell, and for a while she hangs in there, my princess … besties. We do craft together, go to the nail salon, I plait her hair like Elsa's before school, and we cook cupcakes with sprinkles for no reason. It's a three-day love-drenching … until her fuse ignites. She gets bored of me, nothing is good enough, her nail polish flakes, her hair frays and hello: it's wobbly time. A lamp is pushed off her bedside table in frustration, and she tells me, 'You're not even my real mother.' To which I respond, 'Well, I don't know what all the fuss was about in that hospital on the day you were born.'

A door slams and *plop* …

Fred's turn.

Suddenly, I'm all marble runs and bubble guns.

*

Growing up, I often felt these swings of affection myself. After arguments with my mum, I used to sit on my bed thinking up ways I could do better and win back the love I had lost. Being the youngest of four made me a love runner-up. I watched on as my sister, Sarah, who is four years older than me, got the front seat before me, had her ears pierced, and was passed the keys to her first car. Off she sped, out of the driveway towards freedom, and there I stood at the front door clutching my Rock Star Barbie wondering why I never caught up or came first.

She must be the favourite. Not me.

On the day Sarah left for university, I knew my time had come. I was fourteen, spotty and full of hate. I tried to be good, get the full love load, but the era of 'Mummy's cheerful little soldier' had passed. My time to be golden child flushed down the lavatory just like my dummy.

It was too late.

Even if my parents had tried to favourite me then, I would have thrown it in their face like I had the shepherd's pie the night before. Throwing my dinner had become quite common. At that age, if my mother dared ask how school went, whether it was eggy bread, kedgeree or a chicken Kiev with homemade chips, I pushed my tray off my lap and onto the white shagpile.

'I hate you!'

My childish outbursts meant I never reached a high rank. I was destined to be yearning for love for the rest of my life. I went off to uni to search gutters for the affection I so craved. I found it in booze and sleeping around, dregs of love that swilled around me until I met my husband.

But a happy marriage does not make for a totally happy wife. I am, proudly, an unpredictable woman. One moment

I'm all jolly and full of life, then the next I'm crying into my dinner. I try to be in a general good mood, but tiny potholes appear on the pavement of life that ruin my disposition. It's just that being one hundred per cent there, for everyone, all the time, is too hard. I can't pour in equal measure, which leaves someone's cup half full.

On those days, I stay bed. I hide under my quilt until I can face the world again. Everybody in the house knows to leave me alone, when not to poke the bear. My closed door is a symbol of my mood. They just have to wait it out, wake me from my mini-hibernation the following day with a cup of tea and slice of toast.

'Mummy, I've come to cheer you up. I've made you breakfast.' Nell is standing in the doorway holding a tray. I sit up and she puts it down on my lap. There is a little flower, floating in an egg cup, next to some toast and half a tangerine.

'Mum, I was wondering … who do you love more?'

'I love you all equally, on different days, Nell.'

'Okay. Is it my day today?'

'Yes, as a matter of fact, it is.'

I get up, grab a sequin unicorn bag and we head to the plaza, where I park at an awkward angle on purpose.

Today, I have an hour on my own. The house is still. I make a pot of hot chai, put a chocolate biscuit on the arm of the couch and find a cult documentary on Netflix. I pull the little coffee table over, place the teapot within reach, tuck a fluffy blanket around my feet and press *play*.

Bliss.

Then I bite into my biscuit.

Have I bought the wrong ones? I don't remember getting the nutty ones?

I spit a toenail onto the palm of my hand.

Then another.

Somebody has cut their toenails off and left them on the arm of the couch, where my biscuit has kindly absorbed them into its rippled milk chocolate surface.

I spit out eight and actually feel quite lucky when I see two half-moon big-toenails still lying beside me. There is no one in the house, yet the kids are tormenting me. I open the bin drawer, turn my hand over, and the half-chewed nails, like curls of sawdust, and the biscuit fall into the bin.

The kids notice when I am irritable. My maniacal unbrushed hair and my bulging eyeballs tend to give me away.

'What's wrong, Mummy? I thought you were feeling better this morning?'

'Who cut their toenails on the couch last night?'

'I did,' says George.

'Well, thanks to you I ate them on a chocolate biscuit today.'

They all start laughing.

259

'You what?'

'I ate them. I ate your toenails. You didn't clean up after yourself and they melted into my biscuit. Now you've put me off biscuits forever. I'm not letting any of you go to the skate ramp until next week.'

The smiles turn upside down.

'What, a whole week? That means we can't go down there until next Wednesday, Mum.'

Arms cross, brows furrow.

'I hate you! Why are you so mean?'

'Well, it was you who left your toenails on the couch. And you're not getting dessert tonight either!'

'What?

'Don't answer back!'

Tears drip down cheeks and I wonder why I just didn't laugh it off. Why have I turned this quite amusing story into making my children cry? It's not a very nice thing to do. No favourites now.

As they slouch off, I wonder if there are more characteristics that run in my family than I thought?

Am I a cunt on Wednesdays too?

A Nudie Run

'Mum, why is your tummy so fat?'

I rummage through crumpled thoughts before I answer.

'I'm not fat, Nell. I carried you in there. My tummy is a reminder of how lucky I am.'

I try to make good of her comment, but secretly it stings. My next diabetes test is coming up and even though I feel fit, I know my doctor won't see any changes on the scales.

My weight has always been an issue, something I have worried about my entire life. It's the one thing that is never ticked off my to-do list. (Always too much on my plate, I guess.)

When people say to me, 'You look well,' I know exactly what they mean. They mean fat. I often hear myself described as having a 'bubbly personality'. Which also means fat. Or 'You're looking fit!' That is, fat.

My favourite backhander of all time was a guy I met for a drink once. 'You're the prettiest girl I've ever met … of your size.' I nearly threw my pasta ai quattro formaggi over his head, but that would have been a waste of not one but four cheeses.

I would rather someone was honest and blurted out the obvious: 'You're a few donuts short of a bakery, eh Vic!' or 'You look like a "before" picture.' Trying to lace sentences with false positives is about as sly as serving me chocolate mousse made with monk-fruit sweetener. I know the difference. I can taste the fraudulence.

I'm slightly overweight. I always have been. I'm the sort of fat that makes me feel not quite good enough, but almost. I'm in a fat no-man's land. (It looks a bit like the *Teletubbies* land.) I'm not fat enough to deserve help, yet I am too fat to fit in with what the world (and the media) deem to be okay. My desire to always be thinner clamps on to the edge of my brain like a stubborn barnacle. I can't shift it and I hate it about myself, and I'm worried those barnacles are latching themselves onto my children.

My mum is what you'd call a 'yo-yo dieter'. We had scales (which were always wrong) in both bathrooms at our house. 'Roger, can you check the batteries, it's saying I've put on?'

I went with her to WeightWatchers sometimes. I stood behind her in the queue holding her little booklet and a biro, hoping for a smile after stepping off the scales.

'You've lost three pounds, Maureen. You'll be fitting into that dress for the Ascot races before long. Grab the recipe for the pineapple angel cake on your way out. It's only two points. Next!'

The weekly public weigh-in at WeightWatchers at Pangbourne Village Hall reminded me of the witch trials I learnt about in history. If someone had 'gained', I almost expected other members to shout out from the rows of flimsy plastic chairs, 'Burn her, burn the witch! Throw her in the river to see if she floats!'

But, disappointingly, the only outcome of numbers going up were bowed heads, promises to do better and a trudge towards another week of cheating at portions. But Mum seemed to love it, and bought dresses a few sizes too small, ready for her eventual shrinkage.

'I like getting weighed in front of everyone, Victoria. It means I do it.'

My mum was tiny before she had children, a red-headed bombshell who wore jeans so tight she sewed them on. She's spent her life trying to get back there, back to the girl who saw The Beatles arrive at Heathrow Airport in 1964. But the size 10 dresses were never worn. They hung in her wardrobe like reminders of who she once was.

The whole family was on a diet if Mum was. We ate Lean Cuisine for dinners every night. Their tagline was: *You'll love the way it looks on you.*

Meals were straight from the freezer, into the microwave to heat up, and served on a tray next to a glass of lemon squash. We sat in the lounge watching our favourite talk show with Terry Wogan while eating sloppy chicken à l'orange and turkey dijonnaise directly from the cardboard containers.

In the 1980s, fad diets were everywhere, being shoved down your throat like foie gras, and Mum tried them all. She only ate grapefruits for a week once, and when that didn't work she came home from Waitrose with huge tubs of cottage cheese that she spread on Ryvita biscuits. When that didn't work either, she bought books by famous thin people.

'Liz Taylor has lost forty pounds. I've been to WHSmith and bought her book. I'm going to make us one of the recipes tonight.'

Two hours later, we all sat staring at our peanut-butter-and-steak sandwiches, wondering if the local chippy was still open.

When Mum gave up on the diets, we all went back to normal for a few weeks: fish fingers; jacket potatoes; chip butties; and for dessert, a Bounty from the snack drawer under the oven or a fingerful of McNeil's butterscotch sauce straight from the jar. Mum ate the same as us for a few weeks, no rice crackers or 'lettuce cups' in sight, no portion sizes, no points.

'Drink, eat and be merry,' she said as Dad topped up her drink and she spooned an extra portion of potato dauphinoise onto her plate.

We loved it when she was eating and not worrying about her weight. I thought her body was perfect, soft, cuddly and warm. I couldn't understand why she wanted to change.

But after a few weeks of relaxing the regime, her jeans didn't do up.

'I'm starting the diet again on Monday.'

I sighed and hid Liz Taylor in the bramble behind the shed.

*

Now Mum's words echo around our house, yet it's my voice I hear.

'I'm going to try intermittent fasting.'

'No milk in my coffee for me this morning, I'm going dairy free.'

'Can you get me some leeks and a turnip? I'm eating vegetable soup for ten days.'

My husband adds my requests to a shopping list on his phone.

'Right, so that's toilet paper, dog biscuits, bananas, camel milk and psyllium husk?'

'Yes, and some ground dates.'

'Would you like bird droppings and the tears of an African elephant as well?'

I ignore him, but wonder if elephant tears contain protein?

My husband hates it when I'm on a diet, probably as much as I do.

'Your body is lovely as it is. You're gorgeous.'

Even though he says it every day, I stand, looking at myself in the long mirror on my wardrobe and lifting the flap of fat that hangs over the top of my knickers, then let go and watch it wobble. I follow the contours and curves of my body.

Three C-sections and twenty-five years of drinking Stella Artois have resulted in a stomach that hangs from my midriff like a burst chewing gum bubble.

No matter what I do – boxing classes, walks, all the boot camps I drag myself to at the crack of dawn – my tummy does not get any smaller. It's always there, flapping at me like a crow, reminding me my body will never quite be how I want it to be.

So, I do what my mother did. I start a diet I have no chance of completing. I eat super healthy. Until I get hungry.

'Right John, you're going on the diet with me. I can't do this on my own.'

'Okay. Sounds good.'

His content 'this is going to be easy' smile makes me want to leap over the kitchen worktop, pin him down and scream into his face, 'It doesn't sound good! It sounds fucking awful. Feel my pain, motherfucker!'

But I don't. I continue chopping celery.

I'm married to one of those annoying people who can pinch his own love handles once a year and say, 'I think I need to drop a bit of timber' and then loses five kilos in a week. 'Look darling, I need to put another hole in my belt.' After one salad he's turned into a walking SlimFast advert. I hate this about him and, annoyingly, hate makes me hungry.

My husband is irritating in many ways. He will only get more handsome as he gets older. (I know, right!) His grey stubble accentuates a strong jawline and the wrinkles around his eyes make him look wise and endearing rather than old and witchy like me. As I age, I'm starting to resemble a holiday camp comedian who's spent too much time in a smoke-filled men's club. The sort of face that would have had a regular slot at a Butlin's in Blackpool since 1972. A good face for radio, as they say. I think an evil clown from a fairground might have snuck in my house at night and swapped all my mirrors for warped, distorted ones. I don't know myself anymore. A pretty girl used to stare back at me, not this leathery stranger.

My husband is always happy too. Positive. My husband is the sort of person who has a regular bowel movement even on a long-haul flight, can drink coffee at night, and can eat a cheese toastie without getting stomach cramps for six hours. Nothing fazes him; *everything* is easy. He doesn't change himself for the benefit of others, doesn't worry about the opinion of anyone else. He's one of those super-humans, happy with himself.

Unlike with him, my diets work against me. The moment I start, free cake appears: someone's handing out complimentary profiteroles at the supermarket; a mate's slaved over a pavlova that I 'just must try'; a nice older lady at playgroup has made a perfect Tim Tam–covered sponge cake, a pineapple turnover and Anzac biscuits so syrupy they melt in your mouth. It would be rude not to.

Maybe I'm overweight just because I'm polite?

No matter how hard I try, healthy eating pushes up against me like a pervert on a packed London tube. It gets uncomfortable and I have to get off at the next waffle.

My vocabulary around food is now having an impact that goes far beyond my waistline.

'Mum, do you think I look fat?'

My heart sinks.

'No Nellie, your body is healthy and strong.'

'But some of the girls at school are thinner than me.'

I hold in tears as I imagine her life, waking up every day and never feeling quite enough.

'People are different sizes, Nell. The world would be boring if we were all the same.'

Gosh, I wish I could absorb my own words.

That night, I sit down with my husband just like I did on the day I decided to get help for being a total pisshead, and say, 'I think I need to change the way I talk about my body. It's affecting Nellie. I am going to be a bit nicer about myself.'

'About time,' he says and pulls me in for a cuddle.

I throw diet cookbooks away, I delete fasting apps, I leave the WeightWatchers Facebook group. I start saying 'lifestyle choices' instead of 'diet'. I don't talk negatively about my body in front of the children and I try to tune in to my husband's compliments.

I make this choice sound simple, and actually, for the first time in my parenting journey, it is. I just stop being a dick about myself. I choose to love my body again so that my kids can love themselves along with me. Then I go to the fridge and scoff five chocolate pretzels (instead of an entire packet) without an ounce of guilt.

In the bath later on, I sink into the hot water. I wonder if I can sustain this kindness to myself. What if I pass a shop window when I'm not feeling good, or I turn on my phone and the camera is facing me? How can I feel positive when what is staring back is not what I want? Then I think of the dresses hanging in my mum's wardrobe, the lifelong struggle to be thinner, and I know it's a battle I don't want anymore.

So, I surrender to who I am. A middle-aged woman with three children and a tummy flap.

I pat my body down with a towel and focus on how healthy my body is and how it carries me through life.

Then I stride, naked, into the lounge and do a nudie lap while everyone is watching *Britain's Got Talent*.

'Muuuuum. Get out of the way.'

'Look at my beautiful tummy, everyone! I carried you three amazing little humans in here and I am so proud of my incredible body.'

They all crack a smile and I go back to my bedroom, where I put a few pairs of size 12 trousers, a black dress and a stripy jumpsuit that still has the label on it into a big laundry bag to be taken to the op shop.

He's Been

December

Christmas is my love language: my way of getting love, showing it and, like hot gravy, pouring it over people who don't like it. My neighbours know when it's the first of December because I play carols very loudly, strap a fifteen-foot inflatable gnome to the roof and hang fairy lights on fences, trees, bushes and the letterbox. When I've finished, our house looks like a flammable wonderland.

I was the same as a child. The lead-up was unbearable. My whole year until the big day felt like a very long thumb twiddle. Waiting, planning and hoping.

Christmas was a lot more Christmassy in England. I woke up before everyone else on Christmas morning. I looked out of my bedroom window, it was snowing. A shroud of white covered the garden, and the swing set looked as if an inch of lemon meringue pie was sitting on top. I looked down towards the end of my bed, where a pillowcase overflowed with presents.

He's been.

I dragged the pillowcase to my sister's bedroom.

'It's snowing,' I whispered as I prodded her shoulder.

'What?' she replied with a sleepy voice.

'Look out of the window Sarah, it's snowing.'

She got to her knees and we both watched, mesmerised, as snowflakes floated down from the sky.

'See!' I pointed at the pillowcase on the end of her bed and we both screeched with excitement.

I believed in Santa for longer than most. I was twelve, sitting cross-legged on the classroom mat making paper snowflakes when Mrs Granger said, 'Now, cut along the inside edge … and then fold it open. I'm guessing you know by now that Father Christmas isn't real and your parents buy you all your presents …'

As she flippantly delivered this unexpected news, I remember all the other kids nodding, with smarmy 'yes of course we know' grins spreading across their heathen faces. I bowed my head until my chin touched my chest and watched a tear drip onto the piece of craft paper on my lap.

How could this be? I had seen evidence. Footprints. Bites from carrots. Teeth marks in mince pies. If Santa didn't drink the tumbler of whisky, then who did? And what about the elves? I had handwritten labels on each gift. Was she telling me that my letter from Head Elf Stephen from the North Pole HQ was fabricated? And did this mean my three older siblings had been lying to me too?

I went home and confronted my parents.

'Mum. I'm a bit confused. I know the Tooth Fairy isn't real and I saw Dad hiding Easter eggs in the garden last year, but Father Christmas?'

She sat me down and told me the truth.

Instead of being grateful and thanking them for keeping this dream alive for so long, or praising them for the amazing efforts and ninja-like skills, buying and delivering presents without me ever questioning their supplier, I said, 'YOU LIARS!' and ran up to my room where I aggressively shoved a safety pin through the nose of a Dolls World decapitated head.

I never once considered all the hard work it would take to keep this secret for twelve years. I just thought, *You pair of misleading prats*. And decided to never speak to them again.

Well not until Mum called me down for lunch.

The following year, predictably, Christmas time came again.

'Kids, why don't you all sit down and write your Christmas lists?'

'What for? I know it's you,' I said looking up from my *Beano* annual.

'Well, me and Dad need to know what to get you.'

273

Right, I could use this to my advantage. No excuses now, nothing too big for the sleigh. I sat at the table with a permanent marker and scrawled: *Pony. BMX bike. Treehouse. Go-cart. Puppy.* That'd show 'em. Where's Santa now, bitches?!

The morning came, no snow this time. Maybe that was a trick too and last year they'd hired Gary, the man with a snow machine from last year's Winter Carnival. Wouldn't surprise me. No pillowcases either.

'The big presents must be downstairs,' I said to my sister. 'Let's go.' My parents not only gave us sacks at the end of our beds, they also stacked gifts below the Christmas tree in the lounge. That's where the 'main' presents were.

We ran down in our nighties hoping to see the huge shapes, covered in bright paper under the tree branches. My heart sank when we got there. Small boxes surrounded the base. Not even a Shetland could have fitted inside.

Mum and Dad came downstairs.

'Breakfast before pressies, kids.'

We ate eggs, thick slices of fried ham and drank orange juice from pint glasses.

Then, with a full tummy, I made my way over to the tree. Dad appeared, wearing a wonky Santa hat, and started handing out gifts one by one.

The comments were the same every year. If you got bath soaps everyone said, 'Ooh, I love getting smellies' and if you got a top, Mum always said, 'Don't worry if you don't like it. I have the receipt. You can take it back.' And if you got an old ornament that you recognised, she said, 'Oh, I just wrapped that up to make it look like there were more presents under the tree. Pop it back on the shelf, will you?'

After an hour of *ooh*s and *aah*s, everybody had a little pile of gifts on their laps and Dad topped up his and Mum's glasses with Buck's Fizz.

During the next round of gift-giving, I got a disgusting jumper that had a pig on the front, one of those desk toys that had metal balls that tapped into one another and a *Guinness Book of Records*.

Dad, who was now wearing a jumper with *Gold, Frankincense or Merlot?* written on the front, said, 'There's one more here, Victoria.'

The gift was small, but I guessed it could have been the puppy's lead, or a collar perhaps. And maybe Buster was outside the back door just waiting to bound onto my lap and lick my face while everybody cried and sang 'Auld Lang Syne' like at the end of *It's a Wonderful Life*.

I ripped it open without reading the counterfeit label from Elf Stephen, and sighed when I saw what was inside. With the wrapping still crumpled on my lap, I looked up and said to my dad, 'I can't skip, and you buy me this!' Then I threw the skipping rope on the floor.

I spent yet another Christmas morning in my room after being told I was an ungrateful little brat and to only come out when I had thought about my behaviour and was ready to apologise.

A few hours later, I emerged and tiptoed between balls of screwed-up wrapping paper as everyone dozed to the Queen's speech.

While the house was peaceful, I looked around at the decorations in the room: plastic icicles hanging from the mantelpiece; tinsel draped over the tree, weighing down the lower branches; baubles that had dropped off and were dotted around the trunk; crackers lined up next to festive dinner plates; a candelabra dripped with shiny red strings of beads; and foldout bells dangled from the ceiling. There was paper everywhere. I picked up a discarded name label, crammed with twirly writing:

Dear Victoria, Good year? You've been very good at school and been nice to your brother and sisters. Mummy and Daddy told me that you're the best cuddler and you've looked after your hamster 'Hammie' very well. We hope you enjoy this gift we made for you. Never stop believing in your elf! Father Christmas and Mrs Christmas say hi from the North Pole HQ, Stephen. X

I felt a lump rise in my throat. My parents had gone to so much effort. There were twenty other labels with messages on them, scattered around the lounge. One from Rudolph, one from Cupid, another from the snowman we made last Christmas.

I'm sorry I couldn't be there with you this year, Victoria. My chill-dren were all having meltdowns.

The jokes were as cheesy as the ones inside crackers, but as I read each little card, I imagined my parents sitting on the floor, surrounded by wrapping paper the night before, giggling with one another while they took turns asking, 'What do you think of this?' as they searched for cello tape, scissors and biros.

I collected them all and sat down next to Dad as he slept, a plate with a mince pie balancing on the arm of the chair next to him. Before everyone woke up from their dozing, I had one more glance around the room. Our house looked like a grotto and smelt like a gingerbread man. It was filled with tins of sweets, bowls of Brazil nuts and piles of board games. As I scanned the festivity in front of me, I made a promise.

I will no longer be such an entitled, unappreciative brat.

Even though I knew Father Christmas wasn't real, my parents embodied the spirit of Christmas and filled our lives with everyday magical moments.

Mum called me outside later in the afternoon to look at the snow.

'What's that over there?' she asked, pointing towards the patio.

I looked up ...

Parked on the grass, with a big red bow attached to the handlebars, was a brand-new red BMX.

*

Now it's my turn to bring the magic of Christmas. Just like my parents did.

We spend months planning. We buy a real tree and take gross photos of ourselves smiling as we tie it to the rack on the top of the car and post them on social media, hoping people we don't know think we are festive. We make ornaments and bake cookies shaped like angels. Have a fight over whose turn it is to put the star on top of the tree, write letters to Father Christmas, and John and I hide the 'fucking elf on the fucking shelf' eighteen times, having forgotten six times and been bombarded with questions:

'Why hasn't the elf moved?'

'Did you touch it?'

'Does this mean the magic is gone?'

'Is it dead?'

(I'm going to find the do-gooder inventor of that life-draining devil elf and explain that finding new and inventive places to position the green-clad grinning urchin is interrupting perfectly good reality-TV-watching time.)

I've been shopping for weeks. Pacing the aisles of Aldi, hoping to find stocking fillers. I've been making shortbread, mince pies, wrapping toys and hiding bow-covered boxes in wardrobes. I write labels, in handwriting different from mine, from Rudolph and Mrs Christmas. I even made my own crackers with funny Christmas-related dares inside.

Call someone from the phonebook with a Christmas-related surname and say you're lost in the North Pole.

Give the next person walking their dog past the house a mince pie.

Gargle 'The Twelve Days of Christmas'.

We do it all. Go the whole turkey. Paper hats and everything.

On Christmas Eve, the children sprinkle a line of glittery porridge oats from the front gate to the tray of snacks under the tree, and then John skulks around outside bedroom windows, jingling bells. They fall asleep early and we slip between rooms, gently placing stockings at the end of beds.

I wake on Christmas morning to the sound of feet running on wooden floorboards.

'Mum! Dad! Wake up! He's been!'

It's still dark. I stretch, switch on a light and go to find them. They are standing next to the tree in their PJs, pointing at the presents. I have never seen three happier faces.

Suddenly, all the effort feels worthwhile.

The kids rip open presents, hold them in the air and there are even a few victorious laps around the lounge room. George chokes back tears when he gets the trainers he has wanted for ages.

'Thanks Mum. I love them.'

'They're from Santa, not from me,' I say, frantically clutching on to his youth.

But, after lunch there is a change in mood. If there was a record player in the room, it would make that scratchy sound now. Overdosing on Santa-shaped chocolate marshmallows causes a series of fallouts. Nell tells me the bracelet-making kit 'isn't actually the one she wanted', George doesn't share the remote control monster truck, Fred squashes a snail in the garden and then opens the presents that were hidden in the shed for an afternoon treasure hunt.

I retreat to my bedroom, riddled with disappointment. They are like me after all.

George's voice travels up the hallway.

'Is Mummy crying? That's your fault, Fred. Mum told you to wait until later and that it's mean to step on snails. Now go and say sorry.'

I hear feet.

'Sowee, Mummy.'

'I wanted to watch you open your presents, Freddie. I've put so much effort in and I feel a bit disappointed.'

'What's dishhapanted mean?'

'What I mean is … you can't beat up snails. Okay?'

'Okay, Mummy.'

'Nell, George, come here please. I want to talk to you.'

The children gather around me.

'Before you go to bed, I would like you all to write a list of all the things you are grateful for.'

'Okaaaaay, Mum,' they all say in unison.

*

Once they are all asleep, I snuggle up to my husband holding a mug of tea.

'They did pretty well this morning. It's annoying that the day ended in arguments. It's not fair that Santa gets all the credit for Christmas. All we get is dead snail.'

'Don't worry, they were just overtired,' he says as he puts an arm around me. 'One day they'll do all this for their own kids. That's where the true magic lies.'

'I think George knows. He thanked me for the trainers, not Santa.'

'I thought that too. Do you think we need to tell him?'

'No, let's wait.'

I lean back and take a sip of my tea.

Maybe Christmas doesn't end when you find out Santa's not real … it starts.

'I'm grateful,' I say, 'for you, the kids, for family, but what I am most grateful for is that the fucking elf, on the fucking shelf, has fucked off back to Lapland!'

'Yes! Merry Christmas, Vic.'

'Merry Christmas, husband.'

Just before I turn off my beside lamp that night, I notice the corner of a piece of paper sticking out of the drawer in my bedside table. I pull it out and unfold it. The letters are all falling off the page, but I can read it.

The title reads:

Wot I am Grat full for. From Nell.
1.   That I am helfy.
2.   My famallie
3.   Frends
4.   Peepol
5.   I love love
6.   Get sad – but get throo it

I don't get to number seven because six has me sobbing into my pillow.

I think of Fred, nearly losing him, and how grateful I am to have my three children tucked up in bed on Christmas night, close and safe. That's all I need. They are my gift.

Yes, we will get through it, Nellie my love, we always will.

Left to Their Own Devices

On New Year's Eve we fill bowls with popcorn, lie back on sunbeds and watch fireworks from our deck (the 9 pm show, because reaching midnight is as likely as me fulfilling my resolution to run a marathon). Glittery freckles rain down above us.

The following day, presents need to be put away (and never played with again) and the tree needs to come down (and left in the garden for a year to rot). The only indications that Christmas ever happened are a straggly piece of tinsel that's too high to take down and the fairy lights flashing on the front fence.

'Can we leave the lights up, Mum? They look pretty.'

'Okay, and because you've all been good and helped me tidy up today, you can put the TV on in my room.'

They all cheer and run up the hallway.

'Just a movie! No YouTube!' I shout after them.

I hoover up pine needles, wash the school bags and try to track down uniforms to see which ones will fit and which ones are too grubby. I head to my room to hold a shirt up against George and find them watching a YouTube video of a frightening blue spiky-toothed monster.

'Turn that off.'

'But we love Huggy Wuggy!'

'No more TV or devices for two days. I trusted you not to watch YouTube and you have broken that trust. Don't you remember the story I told you about Nanny Stubbs?'

I tell them about my nan and her brothers playing in the Thames River locks as kids. They used to swim there on hot summer days. One warm June afternoon they decided it would be funny to peg it towards home, shouting that someone was drowning.

'A boy's gone under!' My great grandmother, Alice, ran to the riverbank, where the kids laughed and said, 'We're only joking, Mum.'

A week later, my great-grandmother was offered a bunch of heather by a Romani woman at the local market who whispered, 'You won't be sewing buttons much longer if you don't buy this. Be warned the lies of youth.'

My great-grandmother didn't buy the heather and thought nothing of it. A week later, the local kids ran back towards the house, shouting that someone was drowning in the lock.

'Please come Mrs Stubbs, we can't find him.'

But the trust was gone. She didn't believe them and thought it was a joke. So, she didn't go.

Her son, Joseph, died that day.

She never sewed another button.

*

I hide the iPad in the airing cupboard and slide the laptop under some books on my bedside table. I unplug the Nintendo and take my power back.

Parenting is liberating in this moment. Instead of technology, we attempt a game of Trivial Pursuit, in which all the questions are about Australian TV shows we've never heard of, we play Snap and then have what in our house is called 'Night Fight'. Which involves running around the house trying to thwack each other with damp tea towels. Painful yet fun.

Banning devices feels radical. It's the same feeling as mowing my neighbour's front lawn or giving up a seat for a pregnant lady. It's like we've gone back to the 17th century.

'Maybe we should all get a lute each and learn basket-weaving?'

The next night is not so easy.

'Mum, can we put the TV on?'

'No.'

'Can we play *Mario*?'

285

'No, there are no devices for two days. I told you. Look, I've got the playdough out.'

I turn over a box of plastic contraptions filled with a dried-out dough crust. I spend fifteen minutes chipping bits off with a butter knife and then the following fifteen minutes crawling around on all fours picking squishy multicoloured rain drops from within the lines of my wicker dining chairs.

'We're bored.'

I pack the box away and get out some paints. I squeeze out small blobs onto a plastic plate, fill up some beakers of water and run hardened paintbrush bristles under a hot tap. I look at my front gate from my standpoint at the sink and hope a neighbour's head will pop in and witness parenting perfection in all its self-righteous glory.

Oh yes Jane, the kids love getting messy. Let them express themselves, I say!

When I'm winning, I think about the time my mum was reported to community services by Mavis Mooney, who lived over the back fence.

'Hello Mrs Vanstone. There has been a complaint. We're here to check on the safety of your children. Please stand aside.'

My mum let them in. The clipboard-holding lady and her two henchmen barged past and found us in the kitchen, covered in flour and happily rolling out cookie dough.

'Oh,' said the lady, 'these children seem fine. Sorry to have bothered you, Mrs Vanstone. It looks like you're doing a good job.' And off they went.

My mum always said it was the second most satisfying moment in her life. (The first being a date with Cliff Richard in 1967.)

I hand each of my own kids a piece of A4 paper, a little glass tube of glitter (rookie error) and tell them to paint a picture for Auntie Pat's birthday card. Then I turn my back and get on with wiping the surfaces. They are quiet for about three minutes.

'I can't see, Mummy!'

'What?'

Nell stumbles over, arms outstretched like a zombie.

'I've got glitter in my eye. I'm blind!'

She holds her eye open, stretching it so much that I can see the shape of the ball. It looks like a gobstopper. I guide her to the bathroom where I clean it out, calm her down and manage to convince her that no one has died of 'glitter eye' since an unfortunate incident at Studio 54 in 1976.

We are not gone long.

An eerie silence settles in the kitchen as I blow a tiny speckle of glitter off my finger into the bathroom sink.

We head back to see what the others have been up to.

George has disappeared.

Fred is blue.

Even the insides of his nostrils are covered in paint. It drips from his chin onto a wet table. All three beakers of water have been tipped over and the dog is licking the puddle under the table.

'Right, in the bath. Now!'

My attempt at good parenting means, after the clean-up, I now have glitter in every orifice of my body, a daughter who looks like Long John Silver, a bath with a stained blue rim, and a dog that looks like it just sniffed a peacock's arsehole.

I storm into the lounge, switch on the TV, plug in the Nintendo, and place the laptop back on the desk. I go against my promises and leave them to their devices.

I slump on the couch, feeling deflated.

I hear the soft *bleeps* of the machines. The *boing* of *Mario* and the *whoosh* of an email being sent. The sounds are strangely reassuring. At least I know they are near me, that they are safe … No visits from community services today.

I read a book as they melt into screens.

Quiet.

I give in because being a good parent is hard.

Playing all the time, showing an interest in everything they do, listening to their longwinded stories about *Star Wars*, smiling at every piece of art, cooking food that you know will be rejected, putting the lid back on the toothpaste, playing Snap and losing on purpose, driving to the skate park, filling in forms for school photos, making sure they look smart, helping with homework, reassuring them, making sure they get a healthy lunchbox, that they don't hit anyone with a stick, giving praise all day long … when all I get in return are grunts. But I keep on trying to teach them and mould them into good people who do good things.

Bedtime comes eventually, disputes forgotten by then. I kiss heads and tuck sheets around warm bodies. As eyes close I whisper, 'I love you … more than anything in the world.'

It's true. I do. I love them with every part of me. That's why I keep going, why I keep trying. It's been almost a year since I stepped into that first parenting class. A whole twelve months of attempting to grow as a parent. There's been self-reflection, soul-searching, tears and laughter. I've dug deep into every part of who I am. And, surprisingly, I quite like the mummy I have become. I might be moody, unpredictable, exhausted, impatient, forgetful, distracted and overwhelmed, but I am also determined. I will never, ever give up, on myself or on my children. It turns out that I'm pretty good at mumming after all.

Once they are all in the land of nod, I go into the lounge, light a candle, put on a chanting soundtrack, roll out my yoga mat and meditate for an hour.

Not really.

I go to bed and lie there scrolling through YouTube videos of people being attacked by gorillas.

Stepping on Sandcastles

January

All the windows of the house are open yet it's as hot as a sauna. The unrelenting summer sun is pummelling the Colorbond roof. These temperatures have taken some getting used to. When I moved to Australia, fourteen years ago, I had no idea how to handle it. On my first day I sat on a deck chair in fourty degree heatees hoping to get 'a bit of colour'. All I got was heat stroke and a sunburn so bad my chest looked like streaky bacon. But over the years I have learnt about heat, in the same way you learn about rain in England. You learn to manage life around it – or to sit it out until it becomes more friendly.

By late afternoon, heavy clouds bring a tropical storm, big droplets appear, the smell of petrichor in the air, and everyone lets out a sigh of relief.

When it's cooled down and the storm has passed, I excitedly suggest we head to the beach.

'It's lovely now. Not too burny. Why don't we pack some toys and the sun umbrella and just hang at the beach?'

'No, we want to stay here and watch TV.'

When you live in coastal Australia, a visit to the beach is as common as going to buy a pint of milk.

I march over and grab the controller, point it at the box and the screen goes black.

'Go and get your swimmers on. NOW!'

*

I didn't live near a beach as a kid. I lived near the Thames. You only swam in there if you wanted a bout of Weil's disease and a couple of weeks off school. And if you did go to the seaside in England, it was probably a good idea to pack a brolly, a cheese-and-cucumber sandwich ... and then decide not to go.

Now, I live near a beautiful stretch of sand with overhanging trees to climb and rock pools perfect for crab-hunting. There's a mountain in the distance, an island further out to sea. Stand-up paddleboarders glide across the water and surfers balance on curling waves.

I carry a chair, an umbrella, towels, snacks, water and a bag full of beach toys while the kids drag one boogie board each across the sand. We reach a good spot; I let go and everything falls onto the sand like apples falling from a tree. We spread out our towels and I unfold the chair I will not get to sit in. At least it looks nice.

Fred runs off and I wander along the shoreline after him. The other two race towards a dead fish. I'm unaware for a moment. All I hear is the ocean lapping at my feet and wind swishing the long grass on the top of the sand dunes. I watch the children from afar poking a stick at the fish. They're playing. Being nice to each other. And for a second … my shoulders drop. I close my eyes and turn towards the sun.

*

'Is that your child?' An angry lady points at Fred.

'Yes. What's he done?'

'He's been stepping on sandcastles.'

'Oh, okay. Sorry about that. Would you like him to stop playing with your kids now?'

'Yes please.'

I place my hands on Fred's shoulders and steer him in the opposite direction. I send Fred off to play with the others and, as I watch them, my mind flicks back to a memory of my honeymoon in Bali.

*

I was three months pregnant with George, on a beach observing a lady in a stripy linen shirt down by the water. Her two young children were walking along the shoreline where little waves had left a line of broken shells for them to collect. Every few minutes a little hand slipped into hers, the children came and went, showing her their shells. She inspected each one and either threw it towards the ocean or slid her hand into the pocket of her shirt.

I sat there, taking it in, envisioning the sort of mother I would be. Wondering if I would be like her, with kids dancing around my ankles as I walked on the beach.

When her kids finished the shell hunt, they got buckets and spades from a beach bag. The little girl's long blonde braids touched the sand as she knelt. She filled her bucket to the brim, patted down the top with a spade and tipped the bucket over. She turned out a perfect sandcastle. She pushed in fan shells to look like windows, scooped a moat with cupped hands and lined it with seaweed to look like water. Her brother sat close by. He mixed sand with water and dribbled it out through his fist to make whimsical turrets on top of her fortresses.

What a perfect family.

The lady waved at a man in a straw hat who appeared over the dunes. He was accompanied by a younger child. A grubby toddler wearing a dirty onesie. He swayed from side to side like a tugboat. He didn't match the family. He ambled over to his siblings, put his hands on his hips, looked them each in the eye as if to say, 'the party's over', and then stepped on every perfect little structure they had spent so long creating. He obliterated the lot, chubby feet stamping down like a Godzilla with small, clenched fists. The two older children, angelic faces twisted into fury, grabbed handfuls of sand and pelted them at the pampered perpetrator.

'You little pest. You've ruined our castle!' said the older boy as he blinked grains of sand out of his eyes.

They leapt at one another and rolled around on the beach like pythons in a potato sack. Red faces came up for breath between punches, the sand transforming each child into a crumb-covered fish finger as the battle wore on. A sandstorm of tears, thumps and a nasty face scratch led the parents to drag the two older children out of the epicentre of the brawl and down the beach in opposite directions, as the infantile destroyer smirked on a pile of wet sand.

My hand rested on my baby bump as I pondered the situation playing out before me.

This is not a perfect family at all. These kids are out of control! This mother has no idea what she is doing! I'm never going to be like that. My kids will never step on sandcastles!

*

And now, here I am, Fred having abolished every sandy structure in his path.

Before I had children, I thought you just popped them out and moulded them into who you wanted them to be. I thought I had a choice how my kids turned out. They would appreciate the beach, hold doors open for people, eat all their peas and join the local chess club. I thought if I did a good job, they would listen, never answer back and help each other with homework. As I think about the family on the beach that day in Bali, I feel guilty. I had judged that mum straight away. Presumed it was her fault that her kid was acting out and being mean. I had blamed her.

'Sorry, lady in Bali,' I say under my breath.

'Nell, George, we're going to head off in a bit. This is a five-minute warning.'

'We don't want to go home, Mum. We love the beach!'

Nell is sliding down the sand dunes on her boogie board. George walks along a log like a balancing beam. Fred has a pointy seed pod that looks like a pen and is kneeling, drawing circles in the sand. It ends up being a lovely afternoon, and we pack up just as the sun dips behind the horizon.

At dinner, all three kids are lined up along the benchtop, each with glowing cheeks and dribbly noses from playing in the ocean.

'Mum?'

'Yes, George.'

'Can we go to the beach again tomorrow?'

'Yes, but only if Fred promises not to step on any sandcastles.'

'You know that's not going to happen don't you, Mum?'

'Yes, George … I know.'

Epilogue

After our day at the beach, I'm in bed with a warm quilt over my legs, thinking about a title for this book. Dinner is done, and the kids are watching a film in the lounge about a dog that rescues a little girl. I can hear my husband emptying the dishwasher, and soon the bedtime call will reverberate around the house. Teeth will be cleaned, pyjama tops will slip over little heads, glasses of water will be placed on bedside tables. I will read Fred the book about losing a meatball and John will sing 'You Are My Sunshine' to Nell as she falls asleep. And he will fall asleep with her. George will stay up with me and we will snuggle and watch the start of a scary shark movie together. The house will be quiet by 9 pm, the long day transformed into stillness as my family sleep softly around me.

I open my laptop.

So, what is this book really about? A transformation or a failure?

Fingers hovering over the keyboard, I reflect on the past year. Every step I've taken has shaped me. I learnt to discipline without shouting, found unexpected friendships and grew fitter, more patient and kinder to myself. I survived the scare of Fred nearly dying, let go of some control in therapy, and even carved out precious time alone. All of it strengthening my parenting. I embraced the traits I once saw as flaws, reclaiming them as part of who I am.

When I originally sat down to write this, I knew I wanted to tell the truth and share the reality of being a mum. I hoped people could get some tips and learn from my mistakes. I wanted to be the triumphant protagonist of my own story and blossom into the bliss-ball-excreting earth mother I believed resided within.

But the end result is not what I expected.

This past year wasn't about becoming a perfect parent – it was just about showing up, continually trying and forging forward. Every misstep and failure made the wins much more meaningful.

This book is an acknowledgement of what we give, what we give up, how we cope and how we survive.

I tap the letters out on my keyboard.

M-u-m-m-i-n-g

As they grow older, I hope my children will understand what it's like being a parent and realise that the ups and downs are just part of our journey. As Nell so wisely put it: *Get sad – but get throo it.*

Right now, as I write, the kids are doing great. Nell has stopped tattooing her friends, but wapples often. She has joined chess club, a dance group and is auditioning to be in the school play. She also managed to get five stars on her rewards chart this week and had her ears pierced. It's the first time she reached her weekly goal, so I feel like I'm getting somewhere.

Fred is enjoying school, has started football and has not stamped on anyone's sandcastles for a while, and George ... well, he has just finished the course of therapy. It's helped. Even though I notice him keeping an eye on his little brother, I can see he's not letting the anxiety take over. He breathes it out and manages his fears. The maturity he has shown by going to therapy is a sign he is growing up. There are hairs on his legs, Lynx deodorant on his shelf and he seems to have uncovered some empathy for me as a mum.

'It's not fair that you have to go through this, Mum. You not only have to give birth to us, which must be awful, you also have to worry about us until we leave home. What do men do?'

'They take the bins out, pay the electricity bill and do the washing up. It all works out in the end,' I lie.

He's right though. I do worry way too much. It's in-built. But John and I have created a balance between us. I rely upon his stability, and he relies upon my concern. It makes us a good team. I might even hang out some washing one day.

At the beginning of the year I thought I was failing as a mum. I thought everyone else did it better than me, but since laying it all out here in words, I've realised it is okay to get it wrong. I'm still sometimes chaotic and slightly on edge. But overall I'm happy, and happiness rubs off.

I know if a stranger peered through my kitchen window, briefly, they would think, *What an absolute mess! This woman needs help! Why is there a child upside down in a washing basket and another glue-gunning their face to a table?*

To an outsider, my home must seem like an utter mess … but if that person stayed for just a minute, they'd see beyond the piles of washing, the dishes in the sink and the word *ballbag* written in permanent marker on the fridge door. They would see love. Unconditional love. It's the same love I felt standing on the side of the road in France, waiting for my parents to return, all those years ago.

Unconditional love is the scaffolding of my life. Propping me up and keeping me secure. I didn't even know it existed until I had children of my own, but now I'm building the same walls myself, brick by brick, fail by fail, one lesson at a time.

I push the quilt off my legs and tiptoe around the house while everyone sleeps. I sneak in. Soft kisses on silky skin. It's in these quiet moments that I find that place again. The same place I found in Italy, the space between my children and me. I run a bath, add some bubbles, dim the lights, and as I get undressed something falls from my shorts and onto the bathroom floor. As soon as I see what it is, I think about the lady on that beach in Bali so many years ago.

I know then, that even though some days are challenging … I have everything I have ever wanted.

Hands to hold and a pocket full of seashells.

Acknowledgements

I would like to acknowledge all the mums out there. Like most mums, I bear the scars of parenting, not just the line across my gut, but underneath my skin where the world can't see them. This book is for you: the mums who never stop, the mums who take on so much and get little in return. Every single day we get up and hand ourselves over. We choose them over us, them over everything. It's life-affirming and soul-destroying all at once. Just remember, it doesn't have to be perfect for it to be okay. It's true what my friend said: 'Sometimes parenting is fucked.' Even though some days the parent-ship is sinking, at least we're all going down together.

A huge thanks to all the mummy mates I have made throughout my parenting journey. Tears at mothers' meet-ups, spare packets of wipes at playgroup, shared lifts to school, babysitting swaps, extra snacks in nappy bags, emergency drop-offs, understanding nods about sleep, post-baby-blues hugs, communal breakdowns, revitalising walks and laugh-out-loud mum lunches have been the backbone of my parenting. Just having people around me who 'get it' has been enough to keep me sane.

Dear George, Nell and Fred, I'm sorry to say that I've written a book in which I expose all our family failures. I blame myself. I've not written this book to get back at you for dirty plates under your bed, I've done it because I want you to never forget how magical you are. What fun we have, and even though it isn't always perfect, I will never give up. I love you with all my heart. (Equally, on different days.)

A big thanks to my husband, 'Poor John'. I couldn't do anything I do without him. His days are as full as mine, he cleans windows while I podcast, he cooks dinner if I have an event, and he showers me in endless compliments even when I've been in a dark mood all day.

Our lives are so busy right now. There aren't many date nights, weekends away or cosy movie-watching nights, curled up on the couch. We don't even eat breakfast together. We just say good morning, discuss lifts, schedules and forms, then steal a kiss before the school run. We back out of the drive, in separate cars, hoping to meet again at the end of the day for a chat before we both pass out. We both know this is not our time. It's theirs. Ours will come. There's a secluded beach hut in Thailand with our names carved inside a heart above the door.

To my amusing, eccentric, caring, supportive and forgiving parents. I just want to say thank you for your unconditional love. I didn't need words or constant reassurance growing up because I felt it, I fell back on it, and now I've passed it on.

I must mention sobriety here. I tried not to harp on too much about it in this book (you'll have to read my memoir *A Thousand Wasted Sundays* to find out about all that stuff), but I'm coming up to seven years without a 'mummy wine'. I would not be sitting here writing without my choice to quit alcohol. It allowed me to follow my passions and uncover a life I never knew was possible. Sobriety means I get to live life authentically and work on my mistakes, instead of drowning them out. And of that, I am very proud.

I would also like to say a huge thanks to Hamish, my *Sober Awkward* podcast buddy, always there with a smile and positive quote to lighten up my days. What a lovely family you and Liz (best beta reader ever!) have created. (But Hamish, please … Ditch the mankini before Sonny turns thirteen.) I also want to thank Anita and Jack and the rest of my Cuppa Community for always lifting me up and sharing your lives on this amazing platform. You have no idea how much your stories inspire me, each and every day.

Thanks to my local school for the free parenting classes that shaped my year. Scott and my morning boot campers for always making me belly laugh. Nat and the other Hit House boxers for egging me on, the writing group for hearing me out. To my family: Wellers, Vanstones and Wigmores – thanks for being great parenting role models. Flat-Nanny for taking the reigns when I went to Italy and my 'shiny diamond' friends, for being such brilliant supporters of what I do. Oh and Sandy, for being the best dog in the world, but please stop trying to bite the hot delivery guy.

I would not be able to do any of this writing without the support of some wonderful people in my life. Gina, my friend, guide and editor, who prompts my words, eases my fears and makes me laugh. Katherine Hassett, from Pantera Press, who answered all my silly questions and wisely edited out my poop jokes. Tom, Kirsty, LinLi and the team at Hardie Grant for all your hard work, and Sarah McKenzie, my agent, who has believed in me since my first tatty manuscript. All these incredible people are a pleasure to work with and I couldn't feel more privileged or supported when scribbling down all my stories.

Lastly, a big thank you to you, for reading my book. I hope you read it with no interruptions, with your feet up, a hot cuppa and a big slice of chocolate cake to keep you company. But, if you're a mum, I know the likelihood of that is slim. So, thank you for pausing between work, chores and everything else. If this book gives just one mum five minutes of peace on a toilet, then my job here is done!

A hilarious and heartfelt memoir about partying, parenting and sobriety.

'Like a warm
hug with a
dose of humour
– and no
judgement'
*Sydney Morning
Herald* on
Sober Awkward

'Outrageously
honest ...
refreshingly
vulnerable and
wonderfully
witty'
Maz Compton

A THOUSAND WASTED SUNDAYS

A hilarious and heartfelt memoir
about partying, parenting and sobriety

VICTORIA VANSTONE

From the host of the popular comedy podcast *Sober Awkward*

PANTERA
PRESS

SPARKING
IMAGINATION,
CONVERSATION
& CHANGE